EMPLOYEE CONFIDENCE

THE NEW RULES OF ENGAGEMENT

Karen J H

D1069358

Employee Confidence

First published in 2018 by

Panoma Press Ltd
48 St Vincent Drive, St Albans, Herts, AL1 5SJ, UK
info@panomapress.com
www.panomapress.com

Book layout by Neil Coe.

Printed on acid-free paper from managed forests.

ISBN 978-1-784521-32-5

The right of Karen J Hewitt to be identified as the author of this work has been asserted in accordance with sections 77 and 78 of the Copyright, Designs and Patents Act 1988.

A CIP catalogue record for this book is available from the British Library.

This book is available online and in bookstores.

"You can't solve a problem on the same level it was created.

You have to rise above it to the next level."

ALBERT EINSTEIN

Dedication

For My Mum

Who supported everything I ever wanted to do

For David

Whose quiet strength created the environment for this book to be written

For Paul

Who always believed in my writing

Acknowledgements

Writing this book took months. Thinking about writing it was a phase that lasted a whole lot longer!

A chance meeting with Mindy Gibbins-Klein turned the procrastination into inspiration and this book is the outcome. Thank you Mindy, for your process, your positivity, your humour and your belief.

No good book is the work of just one person and I couldn't have written it without the inspirational insights of a special few. Thank you Andrew Lytheer, Mark Holland, David Roshier, Paul Hewitt and Gill McLearnon for your time, your interest and your exceptional feedback when my book was just a work in progress.

Big achievements don't happen by themselves – they require practical assistance and the support of a community. Maidenhead Business Girls is that community, and thank you Amanda Ayres, Sarah Gadeke and Tabitha Beaven for your practical support and advice.

Starting to write and keeping it going takes a colossal effort, and I found myself spending many an early morning, evening and weekend in coffee shops, clattering away on my keyboard as others chattered around me. Writing is a lonely existence and I found great comfort in the wonderfully friendly staff of Starbucks and Costa Coffee who always had a smile for me and took a genuine interest in my writing.

The contents of this book come from years of business experience and some exceptional training. Thank you to David Shephard, Kirsty Mac and Donald McIver for teaching me to think big and follow my dreams.

Writing is full of emotional ups and downs, and I am grateful to all my friends and family for their constant cheerleading – it made a real difference.

And finally, writing takes momentum. In life we never know how and when we inspire people, and thank you Naomi Riches MBE for that story you told me one day because it was that story that inspired my thousand words a day diet!

I am a product of the amazing people around me. Thank you!

Contents

Introduction

This book is about Employee Confidence[1] – a whole new way of looking at company culture and how we engage employees. I am writing it for companies, and ultimately for employees, because Employee Confidence will make workplaces happier, more comfortable and less stressful places to be. Anyone who has ever been an employee in a large company, particularly at managerial level, will understand that the corporate workplace can be a pressure cooker, a stress inducer and a joy zapper.

And the problems don't end there. Even in the workplaces of the world's top employers we see situations that put people or the business at risk, and make employees feel uncomfortable. They know they need to speak out but something stops them from doing what they know to be right. Usually these situations are related to strategic issues with the potential to make or break a company's reputation and its bottom line. Whether it's Health, Safety, Security, Ethics, Sustainability, Corporate Social Responsibility or Quality, a lack of it will seriously impact employees and make the headlines, for all the wrong reasons. You need your people to speak out to ensure compliance and reduce risk, but this requires confidence, both in themselves and the company.

For this we need the right culture, and when we have it, it will drive company performance because both business and personal risk will be reduced. Research studies evidence the importance of culture to performance, and major disaster reports show what happens when an unhealthy culture exists. When we need to address strategic issues in the workplace, such as those cited above, a special type of leadership – change leadership – is required from all employees to

---

1   Employee Confidence – when all employees trust themselves and their employer, exhibit change leadership behaviours and fulfil their potential

build a culture strong enough to drive performance, and Employee Confidence has a major role to play.

Employee Confidence is a win-win for employees and companies. If you have a stake and an interest in People, Culture and Behaviours, then this book is for you. It's neither academic nor theoretical; it's a practical account of how to take a whole new look at your company. For a wholesale approach to implementing Employee Confidence in your company, read the book from start to finish, and then return to the Employee Confidence Rules to help you to put the approach into practice. If simply intrigued to understand what Employee Confidence is, dip into the chapter that most appeals. And if you'd like to discover confidence for influence, for you or your team, go straight to Chapter 9 and read that first.

The value you create through wholesale implementation of Employee Confidence will help you retain and grow the very best talent, and attract clients and partners to you. You will create human capital[2] robust enough to weather the winds of change, and confident enough to lead change and speak out when required. Employee Confidence is an approach to and evidence of culture change, giving you human capital that delivers value far beyond your expectations.

---

2   Human Capital – when employees' skills, knowledge and attributes enable them to deliver economic value and combine to become an intangible asset of the company

CHAPTER 1

Companies and their employees are only operating at a fraction of their potential

Potential is only realised when employees feel confident, and is limitless when we inspire them with a big vision, teach them the right mindset and discover the values that motivate them. Today's companies are only operating at a fraction of their potential because they are not working to develop the potential of all their employees, focusing only on the 'high potentials'. Both company and employee need to become agile – changing course quickly when feedback suggests a better path. They need to learn and grow to reach full potential, removing any barriers in their way and ensuring both paths align. Potential plus confidence means potential realised and performance.

Companies are always on the lookout for talent because they know it is vital to business performance. But is talent the right focus? Shouldn't we be focusing instead on potential? Everyone has potential and it's limitless. For an employee in a large corporate organisation, however, it might look as if potential is something only for the few – that elite group known as 'high potentials (HIPOs)', identified as having more potential than the rest and treated accordingly. They get special leadership training and fast track access to a career path that accelerates their climb up the organisation.

That's great for the HIPOs themselves, but what about the rest of the employees who represent the vast majority? With access to the right training, the right environment and strategies to be able to use their brain more effectively, just like the HIPOs, then who knows what they could achieve?

Focusing purely on HIPOs is a common strategy among today's large companies, but not only is this a strategy that excludes all the other employees, it is also a strategy that leaves much of the company's true potential untapped. It's like finding a bucketload of precious pearls under the sea and never taking them to market. Unless we treat all employees as HIPOs, and create ALLPOs[3] (All-potentials), our companies and their employees are only operating at a fraction of their potential.

This is important because performance is our effectiveness in carrying out a task or function, and the more we unleash our potential, the higher our performance level, so it follows logically that the more employees we have working at full potential, the greater company performance will be. We often discuss performance in the language of market share, profits, sales, and share price, but all

---

3   All-potentials – when all employees have equal potential and equal access to the means to achieving it

of this only happens when the human capital within the company is operating at full potential. And employees only realise their full potential when they feel confident enough to do so. In a nutshell:

Potential + Confidence = Potential realised and Performance

Potential is Limitless and Realised Through Learning

Potential is some point on the horizon which we can all see, and try to reach, and for all of us it looks slightly different. If potential is a point in time, we don't really know when we are going to reach it. Neither do we know what it looks like, and sometimes it seems like an ever moving target. The reason it is ever moving is that the moment we adopt a certain mindset and focus on continuous learning, potential becomes a constantly expanding and growing possibility. As children at school we may discover we have potential, perhaps in one particular subject. And so we work towards realising it – studying for and passing exams, and then maybe even getting into university. Then once at university we study for another three or four years until we reach another potential point where we graduate with a degree. We take a moment to relax, breathe and celebrate, and then we find ourselves a new job. Then our potential point resets itself again.

Employees need the right mindset

The first thing employees need to realise their potential is the right mindset, and we have one of two choices, depending on whether we believe that high performers and leaders are born or made. It may sound like a very simple belief without much consequence either way, but it's a belief that can affect the way you live your life, how it plays out, what you achieve and how fulfilled you feel.

Think about all the high performers and leaders we have in our world – the company CEOs, the executive board members, the corporate high flyers, the sports stars, the Olympians, the bestselling authors – are they just superstars, super talents, who were just born that way, destined to be special and high performing since birth? Or are they just the same as everybody else but perhaps they have just lived a life dedicated to achieving a dream and worked hard every day to get there?

Carol Dweck in her ground-breaking research work and book *Mindset* has differentiated between the two beliefs, with the 'leaders are born' idea being the fixed mindset and the 'leaders are made' idea being the growth mindset. She has also shown through her research that if children grow up with a growth mindset then it becomes a self-fulfilling prophecy – they handle failure and setbacks much better, and understand that success and achievement is not about natural talent; rather it is about working hard, making mistakes, failing, learning from failure and incorporating feedback. And as a result, they achieve more.

Allied to this growth mindset is a belief that anything is possible, and when employees believe this, their potential becomes limitless. What if all your employees had a mindset like this?

They also need to respond to feedback

For employees to have limitless potential, they need to be able to assimilate feedback, so they grow as people regardless of their starting point. We all have the same human capacities, but some employees grow and develop more as people. Why is that? The answer is in learning and the key to learning is seeking out, assimilating and acting on feedback.

Having spent many years training others in public speaking and leadership skills, I know that it doesn't really matter how good employees are to start with because the key to how far they develop is their ability to take on board feedback. Employees who take feedback on board are the real leaders, the real HIPOs, because a) they have a different mindset and b) it sets them apart as 'transformational leaders'. Transformational leadership[4] means leading yourself first, and having a high level of self-awareness and a constant desire to improve oneself (a bit like Carol Dweck's growth mindset), but how many employees and managers do you know that actively ask for feedback on their performance and take it well?

Wherever your employees are in their career, if they want to be leaders and to reach their full potential, they need feedback. That's why coaching and mentoring systems work so well in companies, because coaches and mentors provide a safe environment for learning and growth, and that valuable feedback mechanism. Unfortunately, though, many people get comfortable in what they do and stop seeking out and asking for feedback. They mix with people who have the same level of skill as them, or even a lower level of skill, where they can feel like the 'expert' all the time. Carol Dweck might have called this a 'fixed mindset'.

Some of our employees and managers are open to feedback, but sometimes they don't assimilate it because it isn't delivered very well. The solution is to teach all employees a model for giving feedback and embed it as a standard throughout the organisation. It will change the way employees communicate with each other because it allows useful feedback to be given without any hint of criticism, so there is no chance of anyone being offended.

The feedback model is made up of two simple questions and can be used to comment on someone's performance or to encourage

---

4   Transformational Leadership – a leadership style which inspires others to follow and become leaders themselves, cascading leadership down the organisation

them to comment on their own performance, allowing them to become their own coach or mentor:

1. What was good about it? (whatever it is that you are giving feedback on)

2. What would make it any better? (or what could you do to make it even better?)

EMPLOYEE CONFIDENCE RULE 1 – THE FEEDBACK MODEL

Step one - What was good about it? (be specific)

Step two - What would make it even better? (be specific)

Feedback given in this form is highly effective because it starts by focusing on the things that were done well, making the recipient feel motivated and increasing the likelihood that what went well will be repeated. Then, even more importantly, it uses carefully worded language to make sure that the improvement opportunities are grounded in an already good base performance. This is so important because when feedback is not given well, relationships are affected and the learning is not taken on board. With the feedback model, however, feedback is positive and specific – the two key elements of effective feedback for growth and reaching Employee Potential.

Great leaders give great feedback, in this style, and receive feedback well. In fact, they have probably got to the top of their game, and continue to grow, because they know the importance of feedback and make sure it is being constantly streamed into their brains. Feedback on demand and on a continuous play setting.

They need to be inspired

Even with the right mindset and regular feedback being assimilated, there is still one thing missing: motivation. And motivation comes from inspiration. The key tool for inspiring employees is a vision that offers success and rewards for everyone. A simple example is the star football player wanting to be the top goal scorer but deciding to forgo this in favour of preserving the team formation and passing the ball to someone else to score sometimes. They do this knowing that the vision of being the only team to win the league five times in a row will bring the whole team success and rewards, and far greater than can be achieved by any single individual on their own. In business, this might be a company wanting to be known as the best in the industry for a specific skillset – aspirational for all involved.

Both visions would inspire the team or the employees because they meet the following criteria:

1. Ambitious

2. Long term

3. Towards (worded in terms of what they wanted rather than what they didn't want)

4. Emotional

A vision will inspire employees if it is ambitious and not achieved quickly, because it needs to keep employees inspired for a long time. The language of the vision is also important because the brain is designed to focus on the positive, pursuing what we want rather than what we don't want. The language must therefore reflect this, so we say that we want to be the best in Health and Safety in the industry or keep everyone healthy and safe, for example, rather than not having any accidents or injuries. The meaning is the same but the language is different, and with a significant impact on our long-term motivation.

Probably the most important criterion, however, is the last one. The vision needs to be emotional. This is because the brain makes decisions based not just on logic but also on emotion, and it is the emotion that engages employees around a vision, converting it into a cause that they will act upon and go the extra mile for.

EMPLOYEE CONFIDENCE RULE 2 – CREATING AN ALTE VISION THAT ENGAGES AND INSPIRES

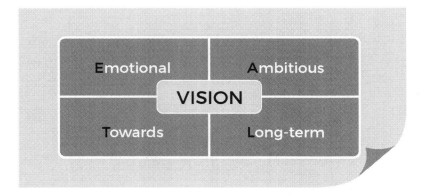

And to know when the plan isn't working

What if you already have an exciting long-term vision? Even then, you still need to ensure your employees keep working towards it. Even with a detailed project plan (and plans) cascaded to all, with each employee working on their own individual piece of the jigsaw, they still need to be able to change course when things change or the unexpected happens. So how do we get our employees to change direction when required, to keep moving towards the big vision? How can we pass ownership down to them for their own progress? How can we give them the confidence to reach their potential? We can't be around to monitor them every minute of the day and give them all the answers. What we can do, however, is give them the right questions:

1. What on my/our project plan is working?

2. What on my/our project plan is not working?

3. What do I/we need to change?

EMPLOYEE CONFIDENCE RULE 3 – 3 QUESTIONS TO ENSURE EMPLOYEE GROWTH

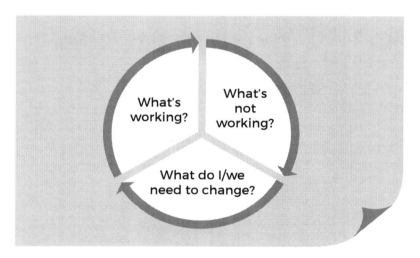

The first question pinpoints our successes, allowing us to recognise our achievements and use them to boost our motivation. It also allows us to factor in more of the same actions that are working and possibly even use this to accelerate our growth even further.

The second question uncovers areas where we can already see a problem or a lack of progress, and if we were to abandon them quickly, change them out for something else, or change course, it would avoid us experiencing unnecessary problems later. In Agile[5] project management terms, it means failing fast and cheaply rather than having to make more costly and time-consuming changes later.

The third question then takes us forward to action, highlighting what specifically we need to do differently, including an update to the plan if required. The benefit of employees asking themselves these three questions every day of course is that the changes required are often very small, if indeed any change is required at all. It stops them spending too much time working in the wrong direction and wasting valuable time, money and energy. It helps them stay on the right path to fulfilling their potential.

Employees Need To Be Coached To Full Potential

To reach full potential, employees need development, based on regular feedback and coaching. They also need resilience, and the ability to coach themselves to withstand emotional challenges, through the asking of the right questions. If an employee can self-coach, they are far less likely to struggle with the confidence they need to keep going.

Starting with where they are now

So how do you know where each of your employees is, with respect to themselves, the organisation and the potential of both? Many large organisations conduct an Employee Engagement survey, using various questions to uncover how engaged their people are

---

5   Agile – an iterative approach to software delivery

with the company, as an indicator of their levels of motivation and willingness to go the extra mile. This is how we assess the 'engagement position' of our employees i.e. where they sit on a spectrum ranging from highly engaged to highly disengaged. What we need to encourage them all to do, however, and in addition to this, is to assess their own 'potential position', both individually and as part of their team. To do so for every single employee would be hugely labour intensive, but some elements can be automated through a regular 'Employee Potential Interview' [6], allowing you to get the basic information, and then encouraging managers to glean the rest through discussion groups and team meetings. And here's the type of information you need to glean:

Discovering what's important to them

To maintain employee motivation and confidence, we need to help them assess what is important to them. We need to discover their values – deep-seated feelings about certain things that are so important to employees that they drive their behaviour. When managers and your employees know their personal values, and those values can be met through their own personal development plan within the company, then confidence and longevity at the company are assured because values are our personal deal breakers. Managers can discover their employees' values by asking a few simple questions:

- What's important to you in a job, or what do you want in a job?

- What would make you leave a job?

- What would make you stay in a job?

---

6   Employee Potential Interview – a personal questionnaire designed to assess what employees need to fulfil their potential

What you are looking for is abstract nouns, such as the words freedom, independence, learning, creativity etc. that could be values for your employees. Usually it is easy to spot these values because the employee's body language will change – they will quite literally 'light up like a Christmas tree'! It's useful for managers to know their team's values and useful for the employees themselves. When every employee knows their own values, they will actively seek out work that aligns with them, since values are strongly linked to motivation.

If you want to keep employees motivated, give them work that fulfils their values. This is far more powerful than even focusing on strengths and weaknesses. And when a team discovers that they all share some of the same values, this can be used to bolster the team as well as individual confidence.

And finding out what's in their way

The corporate workplace is awash with barriers to employees reaching their full potential – from bureaucracy to hierarchy to managerial style. These barriers often stop employees fulfilling their own personal values, even when they know what they are. And sometimes, it's just that your employees are not consciously aware of their most important personal values and need some assistance to be uncovered. Another useful question, therefore, when an employee hesitates, or to encourage them to coach themselves, is this:

What's stopping you from reaching your full potential?

What will often be uncovered then is more values; an employee may say something like: I'm not being allowed to be creative. In this instance, there may be a strong and yet undiscovered value around creativity.

EMPLOYEE CONFIDENCE RULE 4 - DISCOVERING AN EMPLOYEE'S VALUES

What do you **want** in a job?

What would make you **leave** a job?

What would make you **stay** in a job?

What's **stop**ping you from reaching your full potential?

The Company Needs To Grow Too

Successful companies usually have their own models for growth and some also have strategies for ensuring they are a learning organisation[7]. The growth, however, is usually based on profit and turnover, and the growth of people is secondary. The people strategy supports rather than drives the business. What we are talking about here is human capital i.e. putting the people who run the business – the employees – first, and knowing that the business will then take care of itself. Of course, business is all about the profit but it's only the employees, and their degree of motivation and confidence, that can bring about outstanding results. So how do we create a whole company of high potentials?

Starting with assessing our ambitions

Where do we want to be as a company with respect to our human capital? What does maximum potential look like? And do we start with profit and turnover, or a vision for the human capital that drives our company? As mentioned earlier, most companies start

---

7   A company that facilitates the learning of its employees and continuously learns and transforms itself

with the former, although if you were to start with human capital as a goal, you might be surprised at how it drives profit and turnover all by itself.

What is your excellence model for your company's human capital? What would total Employee Confidence look like? What would you see if everyone excelled at change leadership? Where would this lead the company? Asking questions like these will make you see your company in a completely different way.

If you are a company with a major transformation programme, for example, it is useful to start with a vision for the company and encourage leadership to cascade down and through the organisation. Let's imagine a programme aiming to create Quality Leaders, and drive out the cost of non-quality, from the bottom up. In this case, the vision might be to create a company with zero defects.

And if we wanted to achieve a vision like this, what behaviours would we want to see? What leadership behaviours would everyone need to adopt to create a culture where everyone takes pride in their job, works constantly to improve processes, and is determined to get things right first time? When you have the answers to all these questions, you have a model for Quality Leadership in your company, set within your specific context.

Then looking at where we are now

To develop as a company, we need to know our current position, but what are the right metrics for measuring this from an Employee Potential point of view? And how do we collate a full picture of Employee Potential across the entire organisation so we can benchmark our starting point?

Well let's assume that to be a successful organisation, with first-class human capital and a whole company of high potentials with change leadership skills, then we need to measure not just levels of engagement but also levels of change leadership and confidence to enact it, every single day. Your standard Employee Engagement survey (if you have one) might therefore be a good starting point, but we need to trim it down and add in additional sections on change leadership and confidence, making sure we know where our employees are on both engagement and confidence.

Once this Employee Confidence Survey[8] has been carried out, the results collated and independently analysed and fed back to employees, this is your starting point. Firstly, it will reveal whether your challenges lie in engagement (how committed they are to the company), confidence (how much trust they have in themselves and the company and the impact it has on their ability to speak out for non-compliance and injustices), or both; and secondly, where you need to focus your efforts as an organisation to get all your human capital moving forward confidently, in the same direction and towards individual, team and company potential.

What are the variables you might use to measure change leadership and Employee Confidence to enact it? Well if we want to go beyond Employee Engagement and towards Employee Confidence, so we can equip our employees to lead the change we want, then we need some additional questions around leadership mindset and behaviours. Here are a few examples of questions you might ask, with open response fields or as statements with a range of options along a Likert[9] scale:

---

8   Employee Confidence Survey – a company-wide survey designed to assess to what extent employees are engaged, confident to lead change and fulfil their and the company's potential

9   Likert scale – a 5 or 7 point ordinal scale used by respondents to rate the extent to which they agree or disagree with a given statement

1. How clear are you on your own personal values?

2. How closely do your personal values align with company values?

3. How would you describe the mindset expected of you at work?

4. How does this compare to your actual mindset at work?

5. How clear are you on the change leadership behaviours you are expected to adopt?

6. How comfortable are you with the change leadership behaviours you are expected to adopt?

7. What are the barriers to adopting the required change leadership behaviours?

EMPLOYEE CONFIDENCE RULE 5 – QUESTIONS FOR AN EMPLOYEE CONFIDENCE SURVEY

How clear are you on your own **personal values**?

How closely do your personal values align with **company values**?

How would you describe the **mindset expected** of you at work?

How does this compare to your **actual mindset** at work?

How **clear** are you on the change leadership **behaviours** you are expected to adopt?

How **comfortable** are you with the change leadership **behaviours** you are expected to adopt?

What are the **barriers** to adopting the required change leadership **behaviours**?

And finding ways to ensure progress

No plan for company growth would be complete without a regular assessment of the plan, the incorporation of feedback and the removal of any barriers to Employee Confidence. This kind of regular review and adjustment to strategy would usually take place at board level or through some high-level committee. Diligent management teams and directors take stock of the current position against the wider business objectives and adjust the strategy where necessary. These adjustments to strategy then filter down to the next level of management, for consideration in operational plans.

This approach is methodical and rigorous and needs to be part of any growing company's repertoire. I'm not asking you to abandon it. What I am asking is for you to consider it from a different point of view because quite often the barriers are people issues. And when they are people issues it takes someone with a people focus, with a people rather than task-centric working style, to see the barriers and the learning opportunities. It takes a people focus rather than a technical focus composed of analysis and logic, a right-brained rather than a left-brained approach, to assess how to adapt when people are the issue. And people issues are often simply a lack of Employee Confidence.

If you need a company of confident change leaders to take your vision and strategy and run with it, you need to regularly incorporate feedback on Employee Confidence. It makes sense to stick with your regular review and adjustment to strategy, but make sure that the review team includes someone with strong people skills or a representative from one of the people functions in your business. You might even consider setting up an Employee Confidence committee, with someone reporting regularly to the board on the topic of Employee Confidence, based on your Employee Confidence survey results.

Employee and Company Growth Need to Align

Imagine your employees are learning and growing continuously, and your company is doing the same. Both are on the road to full potential, but are they aligned? You can imagine the benefits to be obtained from having both employee and company operating at full potential, and with each employee learning and growing in the same direction as the company, albeit with their own unique needs. This sounds like Employee Engagement but it's Employee

Confidence, because confident employees are engaged employees who trust in themselves and their company, enough to lead change.

Ensure employees buy into the vision

Step one of aligning employee and company growth is in the vision. It sounds so easy – you just write a little vision statement and communicate it across the company, making sure that you stick to the ALTE (Ambitious, Long-term, Towards, Emotional) criteria, as described earlier. In my experience, however, it's not that simple, because:

1. There is a lot of misunderstanding over what a vision is.

2. The vision chosen is neither ambitious nor emotional enough to engage and inspire confidence across the entire company – it doesn't follow the ALTE formula.

I think it's helpful to address the first problem by simply forgetting everything you have ever been taught about writing vision statements, because a vision can have so many different formats and styles, and has been used in so many ways over the years. Once you've done that, we can move on to the second problem, because when we solve it, problem one will simply take care of itself. Let me give you an example.

In large companies, any issue big enough to be the subject of culture change (Safety, Quality, Ethics, IT, Sustainability and so on) requires an engaging vision, but not many companies have visions which engage enough to get their people to adopt new behaviours.

We've already said that a vision needs to be emotional to engage and change behaviour, but what's the secret ingredient? Earlier we talked about a company that had a vision of being the best in the industry in matters of Health and Safety. This vision is not only emotional but also resonates far and wide. Whatever the age, gender, culture or ethnicity of your employees, everyone feels strongly about it because everyone has family and no one wants to get hurt and leave them behind.

Get their buy-in to company values

The ALTE vision described above may also suggest a shared value, e.g. when you are the best in the industry for Health and Safety, it implies a shared value of Health and Safety, based on humanity, caring for people, doing the right thing and keeping families together. But how often do company values really resonate with employees like this? If companies are clever, they include a strong value such as Health and Safety as one of the company values, but many have values that are more transactional than emotional or shared.

For employee and company growth to be aligned, both need to share the same values. The obvious way to do this is through an employee survey to define company values, based on an understanding of what really resonates with employees. This is a good start but is not always effective because:

1. The survey is not worded to uncover what is really important to employees.

2. Employees are surveyed and the results collated but then not taken into account in the company values.

3. Values are written more for shareholders and external bodies than for the employees themselves.

When any or all of the above issues occur, the end result is a set of company values which may look and sound pretty but don't mean a lot to employees. And then employees are asked to adopt them, and live by them, at least whilst at work, but the whole thing runs a bit hollow because the emotional buy-in just isn't there.

The answer is to find at least one value that you know represents a cause and that everyone can get behind, even if it means creating an extra one. One value with full employee force behind it is far more powerful in inspiring confidence and leadership than five official values that employees and managers only pay lip service to.

Find common values for teams

Teams are the powerhouses of companies, and when they are aligned, operating at full potential and collaborating with other teams, there is nothing they can't achieve. Imagine the power of a team of high potentials all aligned around the company vision and values and collaborating effortlessly with each other! Even in the absence of such alignment, teams can learn and grow in potential much quicker when they share some common personal values that become shared team values.

I remember when I was working with the leadership team of a technology company and we decided to spend a whole day eliciting and mapping both our personal and our team values, simply by asking one of the questions mentioned earlier – what's important to you in your job? Or what do you want out of a job? What we discovered then was that everyone in the team had their own unique set of values (we prioritised the top eight for everyone), and even where some team members had the same value, e.g. creativity, the word might have meant something different to each.

What was even more interesting though was that when we came to the team values, many in the team actually shared some of the same values. We looked at which words were coming up for most of the team, and what those words meant to all of us, before agreeing on a set of three common values for the team. Team performance improved, as did their collaboration with other teams, which led to improved company performance.

CHAPTER 2

Disengagement isn't the real problem – confidence is

Disengagement isn't the real problem – confidence is. Employees are engaged when the company's vision translates to concrete action and they feel listened to, challenged, recognised and promoted. Disengaged employees become unproductive – they do the minimum, disrupt workflow and the best ones leave. Even engaged employees struggle to live up to expectations if expectations are not clearly defined and followed up on, and employees lack confidence to adopt the required behaviour. Only employees that are both engaged and confident will become change leaders, feeling confident enough to take a risk, and with a safety net in place.

There's a lot of talk about Employee Engagement right now, but Employee Engagement has been around for years, and many companies have been doing it for years. Global Employee Engagement figures for 2017, however, are down from the previous year, according to the Aon Hewitt report 2017.

Employee Engagement is Commitment to Your Job

If we have been doing Employee Engagement for years, then why are we not very good at it, as the survey results seem to suggest? Well perhaps the issue is not that we aren't any good at it but rather that what employees need to feel engaged has changed dramatically over the last 20 years, whilst companies have continued to deploy the same techniques.

What is Employee Engagement then? There are many definitions but it is related to the commitment to and pride employees feel in their job. According to the research of William A. Kahn of Boston University, it is related to how much of themselves people bring to their job.

Employees feel committed when the company is committed

Employees feel committed when they believe in and buy into the company's vision and values, and this commitment is strengthened when managers' actions reflect this vision and values i.e. when they walk the talk and practise what they preach. If not, all that commitment can be quickly undone, eroding trust, confidence and belief that the company is committed.

A company I knew in the manufacturing industry very admirably established a vision of setting new standards in their industry for employee wellbeing, with a company value of caring and a statement that said 'the wellbeing of our people comes before everything, always'. These words created the wow factor, and the launch campaign created a massive buzz among employees. How proud and committed they felt to be part of such a great organisation that put its people first.

But then as the weeks and months went on, the company struggled a bit to get work and became very cost focused, and employees started to witness manager decision making that put cost before employee wellbeing. One example was in long-haul business travel, where employees were expected to fly halfway across the world in economy class and then go straight into the office for a day's work. The employees started to resent the gap between the visionary words and the actual day-to-day actions of managers, and the commitment started to diminish.

They are committed when they are listened to

Another factor that will affect an employee's commitment to their company and job is how well they feel they are listened to. It is a basic human need to be listened to and heard, and everyone, regardless of job role or position in the hierarchy, has something useful to say and needs to have a voice. In fact, the lower you go down the hierarchy, the more important the individual's contribution becomes, because it is at the lower levels of the organisation where the actual operational work gets done. It's also where the most critical feedback gets heard, through clients, suppliers and other stakeholders, and where the employees become the face of the organisation.

Unfortunately, employees don't always get heard within companies because too many things get in the way. Information often flows well down the hierarchy, but when it comes to pushing it upwards, employees are frightened to speak out. This is often not because managers don't want to listen but that they don't realise that their position in the hierarchy creates its own barrier, and they need to be really proactive to make employees comfortable speaking out and confident of being heard.

One of the best ways I have witnessed of giving employees a voice is through a technique used in training delivery known as Discovery Learning[10]. The facilitator presents an idea, a model, a concept, or a video, and then rather than giving their own opinion, they simply say: What do you think? Or how do you feel about that? Supported by open and welcoming body language, and a long enough pause with kind and friendly eye contact, the employees will feel able, and indeed will dare, to speak out and get their opinions heard.

They want to be challenged, recognised and promoted

As well as being listened to, employees also feel committed when they are challenged, recognised and promoted. Maslow's hierarchy of needs[11] has 'self-actualisation' at the top, being the need to grow personally and intellectually, and develop as a person. I think many people these days are at this level with their careers, and possibly at a whole new level. There is a thirst for personal development like never before, and the advent of the information age several decades ago has made it easier than ever to pursue. Employees need to learn and grow, and get recognised for it. They want to be HIPOs and feel confident that their needs will be met.

This puts a whole new perspective on any conversation a manager might have with a worker. For example, some organisations with construction and manufacturing sites send senior managers out to 'walk the floor' as a way of supporting culture change in a

---

10   Discovery Learning – a technique of enquiry-based learning

11   Maslow's hierarchy of needs – a model for motivation showing that people satisfy different human needs in order of a five-level hierarchy

particular context. The principal aim here is to visibly demonstrate the commitment of top managers to the cause, and it works. It also shows the manager to be authentic and personable, caring about their staff.

There is, however, a whole new opportunity here to engage staff, simply through the conversations that are had during these 'floor walks'. As a manager you could simply say hello and tell the employee what he or she needs to do to comply with policy and procedures, and yes, the employee will listen and respond. But imagine turning this quick conversation into an opportunity to challenge, recognise and inspire the employee, simply with a few open questions asking the employee about their job and how they feel about it. And if you were to finish up with, "What do you think we need to do to turn this into a zero-defect site?" or similar, the commitment will be instantly visible in the employee's body language: they will feel their talent is recognised, and be challenged at the same time to up their game. Now imagine these types of conversations happening throughout your entire company. What would this do for employee confidence?

Disengaged Employees are Unproductive

So even if disengagement is not the real problem, it certainly causes enough of a problem by itself. I mean, imagine trying to run a company with a whole load of disengaged workers. Would anything actually get done? Imagine the colossal effort involved in trying to motivate them to do anything beyond the bare minimum. What if you needed them to go the extra mile one time, with an extra order, an extra shift, or an earlier deadline? How would you get your disengaged employees to up their game when they are only interested in doing the minimum to receive their pay cheque at the end of the month?

They do the minimum

Yes, disengaged employees do the minimum, and they do this because they are just not motivated to do any more than that. We mentioned earlier that motivation comes from values and what's intrinsically important to us, and if we no longer buy into the company we are working for, then it becomes a pay cheque rather than a career. We start clock watching instead of forgetting what time it is and our job becomes a duty rather than a commitment.

And sometimes things can get even worse than this, depending on the level of disengagement. I knew someone once in a previous company that was seriously disengaged, and I don't blame her. She had been moved around several different departments, with no consultation and no support, and felt completely undermined and marginalised. She didn't even want to go into work, she had lost so much confidence, but she had to because she needed the money to support her kids.

With no one listening to her, or even noticing her distress, what options did she have? What she did was take the only option open to her to preserve her mental health and went to the doctors to get herself signed off with stress. When people start to do this in an organisation, the levels of disengagement are like sand disappearing out of an egg timer. Those that appear to be confidently coping are having their confidence eroded on a daily basis, and underconfident employees don't commit.

Disengagement + lack of confidence = stress = poor performance

The best ones leave

The other option for a disengaged employee is to resign and leave the company, and often employees do this in droves when the realisation sets in that the company is not living up to its promises. As a company CEO, when employees do this you might be thinking, well, they were disengaged anyway, so let them leave, they are only bringing the rest down. And to some extent, you may be right.

Sadly, however, when employees resign from a company it's usually because they have other options, of either another full-time job, or setting up their own company based on some unique knowledge or skill they have and can offer to other companies. Whilst it might make sense for them to leave if they are disengaged, we need to remember that the ones that resign are probably the most valuable employees your company has. That's why they have options, and no doubt some other company has spotted this and offered them one. Yes, these are your high potentials but the ones you forgot to classify!

I saw this with a company that had just undergone a major organisational restructure following an acquisition. Many talented employees left in droves, even before the paperwork was signed, and others not long afterwards, under the strain of the intense workload and severe uncertainty. We know that replacing an employee has a direct cost – the cost of recruiting a new employee, plus backfilling their position on a temporary basis while you find the right person, plus the cost of the time it takes the new person to get up to speed.

More significant, however, and often underestimated, are the indirect costs: the unique knowledge that worker had of their job, which is often not documented and never truly replaceable; and the loss of confidence among that worker's network within the company and among external suppliers and clients that the employee may have built up a strong relationship with. Indeed, the employee may take unique knowledge and clients with them, losing the company future business opportunities, and this, allied with the lost future potential value that could have been created by the high potential employee, is a disaster.

And others disrupt workflow

Sometimes disengaged employees don't leave, sometimes because they don't yet have a better option. I say 'yet' because it's only a matter of time. And sometimes it's just because they fear change and lack confidence to leave the company.

Let's assume your disengaged employees stay and the disengagement doesn't result in severe anxiety and stress. What else might happen? Well another option is that they might start to actively disrupt the workflow and their colleagues. They might do this intentionally because of growing feelings of resentfulness. Or they might do it unconsciously out of feelings of insecurity and doubt.

In one company, I spent a week walking the floor of one division to understand the prevailing culture and uncover any issues, in a country where only the local language was spoken in the workplace. I didn't understand everything, so just wandered around and greeted a few people in passing, listening to what was going on and observing the body language very carefully. What I saw was pockets of discontent and moaning and negativity, usually driven by one person within a group and then propagated within it. Disengaged employees disrupt workflow through lack of confidence.

Engaged Employees Still Don't Live Up to Expectations

What if everyone in the company is highly engaged but somehow your people still don't live up to expectations? What's missing? Is it something you wished your people were doing but they aren't? And if it is, what is it? Companies often want their employees to take on more personal responsibility and to show more leadership.

Expectations and behaviours are not always clear

These days we want our people to be leaders, and that is leadership without position power because it means that everyone can be a leader, regardless of their position in the hierarchy, which in itself is a highly engaging proposition. With one company I taught transformational leadership as part of its culture change programme, encouraging everyone to become Health and Safety leaders in a way that created change, by encouraging others to become leaders too. It worked to a certain extent but the change only spread so far. So what was the problem? Well I think we were lacking a clear definition of the 'How' of leadership. Some delegates instinctively seemed to know what to do to be transformational, whereas others remained stuck, not confident enough to try the new techniques.

To overcome this problem, we decided to introduce a coaching programme which gave key influencers (those that already lead naturally in the workplace and others listen to) practical skills in transformational leadership. We showed them how to communicate effectively with all kinds of people, up and down the hierarchy, and suddenly they knew how to do it.

Training is not always followed up on

Another reason why employees don't always live up to expectations is that they may well be extremely engaged through the training they are given, but then when it isn't followed up on, which is often the case, then the motivation quickly wanes and doubts on how to enact the new skills creep in. The CIPD[12] reported on the issue of training follow-up in their *People Management* magazine, citing some interesting research by Ask Europe, a behavioural change

---

12   Chartered Institute of Personnel and Development

consultancy. It indicated that training needs to be followed up on for at least 13 weeks afterwards to be effective, and when this happens, the training leads to real business benefits and value many times the investment made in the training. We can assume then that when training is not followed up on immediately after the training, a large percentage of the learning is lost. And if we only retain a small percentage, then that small percentage is probably also different for each employee, due to our unique brains, experience, thinking and ways of filtering the world around us. It doesn't really help the idea of us all working towards the same goal, does it?

Employees lack confidence to adopt new behaviours

Let's imagine a scenario where an employee is fully engaged around the organisation's vision and values and is clear on the new behaviours to be adopted. Quite probably they agree with the new behaviours as well but something is still holding them back. And we don't know what it is. Often confidence is the problem – confidence to be able to adopt the new behaviours. Employees want to do it but something is holding them back. Or the fear of something.

I knew one company that had a strong value around ethics and this was specified in the company's code of conduct. In fact, ethics and integrity was the cornerstone of everything they did. More than that, ethics was a reason other companies partnered with them and the main reason customers bought from them. But for this whole policy to work there is a big expectation that employees will adopt a certain behaviour, that they will speak out when they become aware of any kind of unethical behaviour within the company, no matter how small.

Sounds easy, this speaking out business, but when you start to work with it, and particularly across borders, you realise that it's not quite that simple. There are many reasons why people won't and don't speak out, and they are deeply rooted in the human psyche or in cultural norms and expectations.

Attempts to change are met with resistance

Of course, there are some highly engaged employees who are clear on the expectations and the required behaviours and only too ready to speak out. Sometimes this is because their extrovert personality allows them to do so, and sometimes it's because they have been trained in communication skills and feel confident to do so. In spite of this, there is a further problem that comes into play here, and that problem is the reception the person receives when they adopt the behaviour. If they are trying it out for the first time and are met with only resistance or criticism, then it's highly likely they won't bother doing it again. This is because as human beings we tend to 'generalise', forming general beliefs and rules for our behaviour based on only one event in the past, especially if there was some pain or discomfort involved.

In the above example on ethics, and the required behaviour of speaking out, I saw the problem for myself. A work colleague witnessed some unethical behaviour and wanted to speak out to her manager. She confided in a few colleagues, including me, before taking her manager aside and telling him what she had witnessed. The only trouble was that the manager wasn't very forthcoming. He acknowledged her point but seemed to be far more concerned with meeting his targets, and told her as much. The colleague felt dismissed and stupid, and resolved to just keep her head down in future.

Only Engaged and Confident Employees Become Leaders

Leadership is often considered to be the sole remit of senior managers in an organisation. Over the last few decades, however, leadership has become something companies have opened to all employees, with the idea that anyone can be a leader, especially when the company wants to create a new culture. And because the only qualification for leadership without position power is integrity and influence, anyone can do it. It does, however, require both engagement and confidence. When employees are engaged and confident, this shines through and other employees follow them.

Leaders know what they need to do

Leaders without position power know what they need to do. They are clear on a specific behaviour pattern to achieve a specific outcome and are personally motivated to do so. This comes from a clear message from senior management that explains all of this and is repeated on a regular basis.

At the time of writing, one of the main rail transportation companies in the UK is running a communications campaign to encourage the public to be vigilant on matters of public security in the wake of a number of recent terror attacks. Knowing that despite a strong motivation for the public to get involved, very often people will still stand back and let others get involved instead, the campaign message is a simple one:

See it, Say it, Sorted!

I have heard it a few times and I can already remember it. It consists of only three words, all beginning with S, and only one behaviour – Say it! So if I see something suspicious when travelling by rail, I need to 'say it' to a member of staff. And the simple message with the sorted at the end makes the difficult behaviour of speaking out seem quite simple! A clever message to encourage all members of the public to become leaders to make sure everyone stays safe, and which clearly communicates the required behaviours.

Leaders are confident enough to take a risk

Being a leader with no position power can be risky because it relies on pure skill to influence. With position power, you can have no communication or influencing skills whatsoever, but people will still listen to you because of your position in the hierarchy, or your authority in some area. And this is precisely why, conversely, leaders tend to rise from lower down in the ranks because they are forced to hone their communication skills, whereas those with position power are not. So why are we giving all our attention to our senior leaders when leaders without position power are often more skilful?

Leading without position power is risky, however, because there is the potential of a leadership communication being received as a challenge rather than a support, and this gives rise to fear if employees don't have confidence in the outcome.

Leaders know where their safety net is

Sports performance is all about stretching your abilities to see how far you can go. It's about constantly seeking to improve your personal best. Doing this also requires taking a risk, as we described earlier, but what if it all goes wrong? What if you end up back in a worse position than you were before you took the risk? In sports this might mean injuring yourself. In business it could mean losing your job. With any risk there is the possibility of loss and damage, and we need to mitigate against it.

We do this by finding some sort of a safety net. In one company I worked with, for example, they had a safety programme which stressed the specific behaviour of intervening and stopping the job should any employee perceive a safety risk to exist, and regardless of the cost of stopping that job. And in hazardous environments like construction, manufacturing, and oil and gas, stopping the job, even for a few minutes, is an extremely costly business, sometimes running into millions.

Against this backdrop, stopping the job, even for the safety of workers, requires the taking of a personal risk – the risk of incurring the wrath of an angry boss or client for example. So where is your safety net and what form does it take? In this example, the safety net was a coaching culture. A critical mass of people was trained in how to give and receive feedback in a positive way, which meant that whenever someone was brave enough to speak out and stop the job, two things happened:

1. They knew how to do it in a way that was clear, confident and instilled trust.

2. The intervention was received in a positive manner.

When we want our employees to be leaders, we need to remember that change leadership is accompanied by risk, and we need to help them mitigate it. When we do so, we increase their confidence and enable them to deliver the results the business needs.

We need four things from our employees today. Knowledge, skills and experience are a given, and with effective engagement strategies we can also achieve their commitment. With confidence, however, and a safety net to support it, the engagement strategy creates not just committed employees but leaders as well. Confidence, therefore, is the critical piece in the jigsaw. Confidence activates potential.

EMPLOYEE CONFIDENCE RULE 6 – CONFIDENCE IS THE CRITICAL PIECE IN THE POTENTIAL JIGSAW

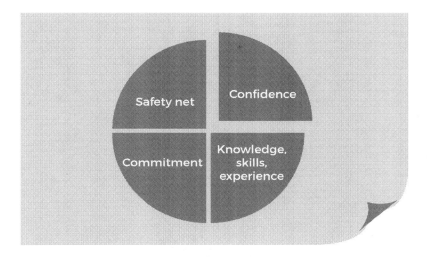

CHAPTER 3

Employee Confidence is good for business

Employee Confidence is the right thing to do because it looks after our people, recognising the unique value they bring and helping them reach their full potential. It's also good for business, saving time and money, boosting morale and company reputation, and preserving intellectual property. It goes beyond engagement because confident employees find leadership easy and inspire others to follow, creating a culture of leadership that enables positive change. And that culture of leadership brings results, due to increased ownership and faster decision making that reduces costs and boosts productivity.

Confidence is a word with many definitions and generally people have different views on what confidence means to them. The most common definition is that confidence is an individual's trust and belief in their ability to do something. And this trust often comes from experience. It also comes from a belief that either there is little personal risk involved or that any personal risk involved can be mitigated. Whichever definition we choose, confidence is always perceived as a good thing, opening doors for people in all aspects of life. Being an employee is tough sometimes. Employers expect more and more of them, so it goes without saying that we need them to be confident, although this is rarely discussed in the workplace.

Employee Confidence is the Right Thing to Do

As employers and line managers we can make or break our employees' confidence, although we maybe haven't ever thought about it in these terms before. We know that we can make or break their engagement, and that is critical to the business, but making or breaking our employees' confidence? Now we are talking about a much more serious matter because confidence affects self-esteem; it affects what an employee will or won't do; it affects their career prospects; and it also affects their personal life. Whatever way we look at it, giving our employees confidence is the right thing to do because it shows we care about them as humans, and not just human resources.

People are the heart of the business

People are the heart of the business. It's a statement you have probably heard before. But let's think about it for a minute. If people are at the heart of the business, it suggests two things:

1. The business has a heart.

2. People are right at the centre i.e. they drive the business and can make or break it.

The first point is important because no one wants to do business with robots. We may be moving into an age of artificial intelligence but people still want to do business with people, and that is unlikely to change, even with the advent of robots to enhance performance. The second point is important because it has serious business implications. We tend to think that people stuff is fluffy and secondary, run by people in support functions who are simply an overhead to the business. This couldn't be further from the truth – people stuff drives culture which drives performance.

I heard a story once about an airline that was having trouble with customer complaints. Every time there was a delay or issue on the ground, customers got really annoyed with the way they were treated. The system to deal with the issue just seemed to exacerbate the problem for the poor traveller. This was affecting company reputation, sales, and share price!

The management couldn't understand the problem to start with because they had first-class customer service people, with excellent training, and some great procedures in place. When they eventually spoke to the customer service staff to find out how they felt, the real problem was revealed. The customer service staff just didn't feel empowered to make little gestures to weary travellers to appease them, like free food and drink, because the procedures were so rigid that they didn't allow for it. It didn't allow staff to be flexible and show their human side, and this meant that they couldn't be the heart of the business even if they wanted to.

They need a sense of belonging

When we are caring about our people, it's not just about looking after their health, their safety, their security and their wellbeing, although these things are important and also a legal obligation. As well as being the right thing to do, employers have a legal duty to take care of their employees, and make sure they go home safely and are not exposed to anything at work that could harm their health, security or wellbeing.

When we look at Maslow's hierarchy of needs, which says our needs have to be satisfied in a certain order, safety and security are at the bottom after physiological needs such as food and water, which we would probably call welfare. When we talk about looking after people's welfare, then, and their safety and security, we are still pretty much at the bottom of the triangle. After these needs come love and belonging, esteem and self-actualisation, in that order, but I wonder how far we really go as employers to provide these?

A sense of belonging is provided by a strong team ethos, a community feel and after-work social activities, and most large companies provide this, although it is still possible for individuals to feel like they don't belong. An example of this is a company that decided to seriously address the issue of gender diversity in their male-dominated workplace, and did this by appointing a senior manager to develop and implement a company-wide strategy. Training was rolled out but take-up was sporadic because there weren't enough female managers at senior level to advocate for it.

If we want to engage certain groups of people, then we need to have a group of decision makers representative of all minority groups. Employees can't really feel fulfilled unless they belong, and once they belong, then and only then can they tune into any self-actualisation activities offered, such as personal development plans and training opportunities.

Maybe belonging is a wider issue than we think? Many companies have already extended the scope of their diversity programme beyond gender, covering all and any minority groups within the business. Not just because it's the right thing to do but because diversity policies help belonging, and belonging leads to confidence among employees to go for self-fulfilment.

Employees are all different

Earlier when we discussed the need for follow-up on training, we said that each individual retains information in a different way, due to their unique way of filtering the world. To say we are all unique and different is obvious, but do we as employers really take this into account? In the Human Resources and Learning and Development functions we learn about people, their learning styles and preferences, and possibly even different styles of communication, but to what extent do we consider this in our engagement strategies?

In one company I worked with, we used personality profiling models within their transformation programme to help employees become better leaders and lead the change. The model showed employee preferences for thinking, working and communicating. Armed with this information about themselves, and about others, employees who sat the course were able to adapt their communication style and connect quicker with others, for better results and win-win solutions.

Giving employees access to a tool like this shows we recognise that everyone is unique and different, and that we are prepared to invest in that. Imagine the culture of diversity and leadership that could be developed when everyone has access to and uses their own unique personality profile, and when it is used in teams and meetings to the extent where it becomes the language for appreciating, recognising and communicating with others! Imagine the potential opportunity, and the opportunity for potential!

Employee Confidence is inclusive

If we can't help all our employees achieve self-fulfilment, then how ethical are we being as companies? Is it enough to provide for their own lower level needs and then leave them to find self-actualisation all by themselves? Well it really depends on what kind of environment we provide for the achievement of self-actualisation, and to what extent we cater for individual differences, as described earlier. And I think we also need to recognise that our workplaces are high pressure, high stress environments, where the pace of change has got out of control and all of us are struggling to keep up. Against this backdrop, we can unwittingly be creating barriers to self-actualisation as fast as we create them.

This is where Employee Confidence comes in. We can cater for our employees' basic needs very well, and give them a sense of belonging, through social activities, a team ethos, and a strong culture of diversity, but still barriers created by stress and pressure can knock their confidence and stop them even seeking out self-actualisation. If we want our employees to show personal leadership, then we must do this in an ethical way and keep a close eye on the environment we are creating. Could we consider it a basic human right to work in a stress-free workplace and to feel confident at work?

A great example of this is a company where I heard that risk was already a boardroom issue and risk management a strong strategic competence. They decided to introduce human rights risk as a boardroom issue, covering all their employees and the communities where they do business, and manage the risk in the same way that they managed other risk. They integrated this specific risk into the risk management system across the company and developed procedures to mitigate and even eliminate it. This was an ethical approach, inclusive of all those involved in or affected by company activities, and I imagine this greatly boosted Employee Confidence across the company.

Employee Confidence Retains Talent

When employees feel confident, both about their organisations and about their own abilities to learn, grow, develop and speak out, then why would they look anywhere else for employment? We live in a world of limitless opportunities and endless information. Different career opportunities are emerging all the time and people are carving out their own self-employed opportunity where they feel confident, as discussed earlier. Even so, many remain in the employment of others, and usually for one of these three reasons:

1. The security of the pay cheque at the end of the month

2. The fear of change and ending up worse off

3. Working with great people and feeling confident in what they do

Now let's look at how this relates to staff retention.

Non-retention is costly

HR professionals know the challenge of retaining staff. It is usually identified as a boardroom issue because it ties in directly to the company's ability to deliver work to clients. This is particularly acute when it comes to those identified as key or critical staff – usually employees in client-facing roles or playing a major role in a project. They might be people with unique skills, or work in a field where a specific skillset is hard to retain, due to skills shortages. They might also simply be those classified as HIPOs.

Whoever they are, what's significant is that they have confidence in the organisation and in themselves, and if they feel uncomfortable in their role, they often leave, as mentioned earlier. And it's usually the high performers or the people in these critical roles that leave because their skills are such that they don't find it difficult to find work elsewhere. We all know that there is a cost to this – the cost of backfilling, recruiting someone new, the time taken to train the new person up, and so on, and so on. And it takes time. But is this the real cost? What about the hidden costs?

We mentioned indirect costs earlier, particularly around employees taking knowledge and clients with them, and a set of questions to uncover them might look something like this:

1. What value is the employee providing right now?

2. What value will they have provided in five years' time?

3. What's the full potential of this employee?

4. What will this mean to the business?

5. Who else values your employee?

6. What will happen if your employee leaves?

7. What won't happen if your employee leaves?

8. What will happen if they don't leave?

9. What won't happen if they don't leave?

These are questions designed to get you thinking about the problem from several different angles, and each yielding a new and slightly different piece of information. Try them out with one of your HIPOs for starters and see what hidden costs you uncover. It's called analysing employee VPMR – their Value, Potential, Meaning and Result.

EMPLOYEE CONFIDENCE RULE 7 – ANALYSING EMPLOYEE VPMR

VALUE

What value is the employee providing right now?

What value will they have provided in five years' time?

Who else values your employee?

POTENTIAL

What's the full potential of this employee?

MEANING

What will this mean to the business?

RESULT

What will happen if your employee leaves?

What won't happen if your employee leaves?

What will happen if they don't leave?

What won't happen if they don't leave?

Retention boosts morale and reputation

The big problem with employees leaving your organisation, particularly high performers, is that it's never just one. There's usually a reason that Employee Confidence is draining, and if your key players are leaving, then the reason is probably a big one. And it won't just affect one member of staff. If only one has left for now, then it's only a matter of time. You can be sure they are all busy looking for new jobs in their spare time and probably in your time, and as soon as they get the right offer, they'll be off. When someone key and well-respected in the company announces they are leaving, it sends something akin to confidence shockwaves through the ranks.

High long-term retention rates are a pretty good indicator of Employee Confidence, and we all know that success breeds success, so the more staff are retained, the more they are retained, if you know what I mean. In the same way that losing employees starts to spiral, retaining them does the same thing to morale but in reverse. When people aren't looking for other jobs they have more time and energy to devote to their work.

I knew someone once in a technology company, and he was the key person in the team, the ideas guy, coming up with all the new concepts. All his great ideas were then being sold on to the company's main client, and this boosted company reputation in the industry. And then he left, taking all his great ideas to another company. Imagine the lifetime value of that future revenue stream for the company – all lost! You can replace an employee but you can't replace that special something that some employees have, that unique brain power based on unique experience in the world, and the way they contribute to company reputation.

Employee Confidence goes beyond Engagement

What is it exactly about Employee Confidence that makes the difference? Don't we just need engagement from our employees to keep them? Well we said earlier that confidence was about the trust an employee has in himself or herself, and in the company. It's also about belief. What does each employee believe about their role in the company? Do they believe in the company's values and mission? Do they believe in their unique role in that mission? Do they believe they can make a difference? And do they believe in themselves? Ultimately, an employee's answers to these questions, i.e. whether they have a combined belief in both themselves and the organisation, is going to impact the extent to which they stay with the company in the long term.

Another important factor is capability. How capable are your employees in delivering on these beliefs? Are they capable of doing what the company needs them to do to make that difference and to fulfil the role expected of them? And even if they started out capable, today's organisations have ever increasing expectations of their employees, in an environment of change, growth and economic and political uncertainty, so these capabilities get stretched, sometimes with unrealistic expectations. Are your employees capable of being the change leaders you expect them to be?

When we combine belief with capability we get confidence, and that's what we need for our employees. Let's consider this formula:

BELIEF + CAPABILITY = EMPLOYEE CONFIDENCE

We can use a simple 2 x 2 model like the one in diagram 1 below to assess our company as a whole, and different parts of the business, on Employee Confidence. It's a simplistic model but the two elements of belief and capability can be broken down further in your regular Employee Engagement (now Employee Confidence) surveys. And I wonder how your employees would feel knowing that you are now not just interested in their engagement but want them to be confident as well? Confident, perhaps!

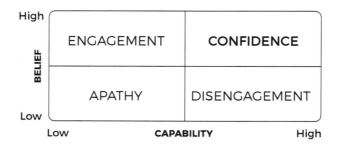

Diagram 1

EMPLOYEE CONFIDENCE RULE 8 – BELIEF + CAPABILITY = CONFIDENCE

Low belief + low capability = apathy

Low belief + high capability = disengagement

High belief + low capability = engagement

High belief + high capability = confidence

Employee Confidence Promotes Leadership

So, if belief plus capability means confidence for employees, where does confidence lead? If you really believed in yourself and the company, and felt really confident in your role within the company and your own abilities, how would you behave? This is an excellent question, because in my experience, confident employees behave as leaders, and without prompting from management. In fact, they embrace a particular type of leadership – change leadership.

Confident employees become change leaders

Confident employees behave as leaders and that means feeling, looking and sounding like leaders. They have bought into a particular mission or cause within the organisation, know what is expected of them and feel comfortable exhibiting the required behaviours. They exude positivity and authenticity because they are comfortable in their own skin and take personal responsibility for making things happen, despite resource constraints and the daily obstacles and barriers of the workplace.

In one company for example, management introduced a leadership programme which encouraged everyone to become leaders for occupational health and hygiene. The aim was that if everyone bought into the idea and adopted the required behaviours, it would create a culture where employees put health and hygiene first – a critical issue in some industries.

One behaviour required was for workers to intervene and stop the work if they should ever perceive there to be a risk to the health and hygiene of their employees and those affected by their work. With the training they were given, some employees started intervening straight away. Others still needed a bit more confidence to make the change. The ones that really excelled, however, were the volunteer trainers from within the company that were recruited to deliver the leadership programme.

Their belief was stronger than that of the other employees, which is why they volunteered in the first place. They also had a higher level of capability, since they had received an advanced level of training in the programme tools and techniques through the process of becoming accredited trainers. This led them to confidently take their leadership skills out into the workplace and to teach them to others. Seeing this showed me that if you combine a strong enough belief with sufficient capability you get confidence that leads to change leadership – ambassadors for a cause.

Leaders create culture

What makes some employees lead when others prefer to follow? Well the answer might be in personality traits, and according to Jungian[13] psychology, we all have 72 archetypes within us that represent personality traits that we all can access. So, should we choose to access the 'ambassador' trait, for example, we would

---

13   Carl Jung – Swiss psychiatrist whose work emphasised the individual psyche and the quest for wholeness

demonstrate a high level of social intelligence with charm and strong listening skills. That would be useful for leading change, wouldn't it? Yes, I think so, but not all of us are comfortable accessing certain personality traits and prefer to stick to the few we are comfortable with.

Despite having all 72 archetypes within us, not all of us are natural leaders. We can, however, develop the capability and we are more likely to do so once we have the belief. In the example above, the volunteer trainer pool developed to support the health and hygiene leadership programme emerged as natural leaders and ambassadors because of the growing confidence they got from combining belief with capability.

Confidence allows employees to act in line with their values and beliefs because they have the capability to do so, and there is nothing more inspiring than someone acting in line with their values and beliefs. When employees do this, they come across as charismatic and authentic, and when at the same time they start to listen more to others, pay other employees individual attention and ask clever questions to challenge their thinking, this becomes 'transformational leadership'.

Transformational leadership has a very interesting outcome. Since the new leaders start to inspire others with this type of behaviour, others follow them. And not only do they follow them but they start to adopt the same behaviours, become leaders themselves and contribute to culture change.

This is exactly what happened with the health and hygiene leadership programme described above. The volunteer trainers sparked off a whole wave of new leaders who became advocates of following the health and hygiene rules, intervening to ensure everyone did so, and promoting regular and inclusive conversations on health and hygiene before the work started every day. When this reached critical mass after about four years, it became a visible health and hygiene culture, and measurable through a regular survey.

Leadership Brings Results

Why should we worry so much about leaders? Why would we want so many leaders in our companies anyway? Don't we already have enough at the top of the hierarchy? Won't having a whole army of leaders be counterproductive? In fact, it's exactly the opposite, because this isn't leadership as we know it, for the upper echelons of large companies. No, this is leadership without position power, and to make it work, the employee has to be even more skilful at it precisely because they have no formal authority. As described above, a critical mass of employees showing leadership creates and changes culture, and culture change is inevitable if the company wants to grow and reach full potential.

Culture change has been linked to performance in many arenas. Barling et al., for example, carried out research in the food industry in 2002, and the result simply confirmed the results of other research that linked culture to performance, only in this case it was safety performance. They discovered that when a good safety culture is created, through transformational leadership and the improved safety awareness that brings, then the end result is a reduction in occupational injuries and incidents i.e. enhanced health and safety performance.

It increases ownership and accelerates decision making

How does culture drive performance and where does leadership fit in? The first thing leadership does is increase ownership out on the ground, at grass roots level, empowering employees to take responsibility and make faster decisions. In fact, ownership is a key element of leadership, but how far do you allow employees to go? If they take ownership of everything, they start to work outside systems and procedures, all of which have been put in place for very good reasons. What we are talking about here is the delicate balance between compliance and ownership, particularly in large organisations that require systems because of their size and formal nature.

In diagram 2 below we see another simple 2 x 2 model that allows us to understand the interplay between compliance and ownership, and what it leads to. It also allows us to understand leadership a little bit better. In the matrix below, we consider the variables of ownership and compliance, and their low and high variants, to see what happens in each of the four potential combinations.

EMPLOYEE CONFIDENCE RULE 9 – OWNERSHIP + COMPLIANCE = CHANGE LEADERSHIP

Low ownership + low compliance = chaos

Low ownership + high compliance = group think

Low compliance + high ownership = innovation

High compliance + high ownership = change leadership

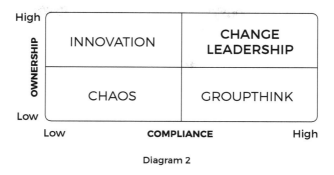

Diagram 2

When we have low ownership and low compliance, we get chaos. The rules aren't followed and the employees just don't care about it, or doing anything about it. When we have low ownership but high compliance, we are in danger of getting 'groupthink'[14], where employees just follow the most dominant line of thinking. With low compliance and high ownership, we get innovation from our employees, something that most CEOs would like a little more of in their companies. But whether this innovation is a good thing or not really depends on how comfortable you are with them breaking the rules. If it's a team set up exactly for this purpose, then that's a different matter.

Ultimately what we want is both high compliance and high ownership from our employees, and for them to innovate and work independently to solve problems whilst at the same time referring back to the overall management system with its rules and procedures. When we achieve this, we have change leadership, and this drives culture change and performance.

---

14   Groupthink – a phenomenon whereby pressure to conform within a group hinders rational decision making

It reduces costs

Leadership reduces costs when CEOs inspire their people to do exactly this – to work within the overall framework of systems and procedures whilst at the same time taking ownership of problems on the ground and solving them. Ideally, we want them to go one better and to take personal responsibility for making sure they and their whole team stick to the system and procedures and fix any non-compliance, or any problem with the existing system, themselves. When problems are solved on the ground, without being referred upwards or across the organisation to a different function, it saves time and money.

In one company I worked with, we decided to establish three clear behaviours for this kind of leadership, with the aim of improving the safety culture across the organisation. The idea was that if everyone adopted these three behaviours, we would have a company of safety leaders and the safety culture would improve greatly, keeping everyone safe in what was a dangerous working environment and boosting safety performance.

We chose one behaviour that set an example to others, one which promoted two-way communication around the topic, and another that empowered employees to express their feelings and report any at-risk situations in the workplace.

EMPLOYEE CONFIDENCE RULE 10 – KEY "E" BEHAVIOUR TYPES FOR CHANGE LEADERSHIP

A behaviour that sets the example for the ideal (**EXAMPLE**)

A behaviour that improves communication around the topic in question (**EXCHANGE**)

A behaviour that empowers employees to express their feelings and report at-risk situations (**EXPRESS**)

The first behaviour is about compliance and this is the first element of leadership with or without position power. It means leading by example, walking the talk. The second behaviour is getting others to talk about the topic you want everyone to lead on, leading to vital pieces of information being discovered, and in this case, safety-critical information. The third and final behaviour is taking personal responsibility for acting on that information. All three lead to ownership within a shared framework of compliance, reducing costs as workers become autonomous problem solvers.

It drives productivity

When we devolve leadership down to grass roots and ask for certain behaviours, we get the culture we are looking for. As well as encouraging compliance and ethics, it also drives productivity, because when employees follow the rules, things go right. Problems arise when people take shortcuts, because then incidents and errors start to happen, and the costs of injuries, insurance claims, re-work and downtime can be extortionate. Leadership for any strategic issue then is almost always used to ensure compliance. When we do things right the first time i.e. according to the Standard Operating

Procedure, we avoid the costs of waste, duplication, downtime and health and safety incidents, and are therefore more productive.

There is another added benefit to this type of leadership. Imagine the example described above, in the company where efforts were made to improve safety culture. Employees were surveyed on their engagement levels and the extent to which they worked safely, and something very interesting was uncovered. It seemed that when they worked safely and everyone around them did the same, purely because the safe way had also been engineered to be the quickest way, they felt better. They felt safer, so they were more confident, and this made them more productive. If we want our employees to fulfil their potential and act in a certain way, we need to create the right environment in our workplaces.

CHAPTER 4

Employee Confidence creates the environment for peak performance

Employee Confidence creates the environment for peak performance. Employees feel valued because their managers notice them as individuals, support their aspirations and recognise their achievements. They feel listened to, know their voice is important and see how their ideas are actioned. Line managers encourage employees to have personal as well as business goals and support them to stretch their capabilities. Above all, employees work in teams where they feel supported, championed and understood. All of this makes for confident employees and a confident organisation.

We have started to think about what confidence means within an organisation, both to employees and to the company. We have also looked at creating leadership throughout the organisation, where employees feel confident enough to take on that role, and the benefits that this leadership brings. This confidence among employees is contagious and leads a culture that drives results and performance.

There is, however, a deeper element to confidence and it's about honesty and trust – an employee's trust in their own abilities and in the company to support them. Have you ever busied yourself preparing for an important meeting or presentation and worried more about the politics in the room than the presentation itself? When you work in an honest working environment, these worries become a thing of the past.

Employees Feel Valued

There are several elements to an honest working environment and all of them create Employee Confidence, both individually and collectively. The first one is employees being, and feeling, valued, and this is broken down into three areas as follows:

Managers treat them as individuals

Employees are individuals. And each of us is uniquely different from the rest. So why do we treat employees as one homogenous unit? Apart from the HIPOs that is. The answer is probably in the resources it takes to treat every employee differently but this might be easier than we think. With the right framework that allows for personalisation by managers, we can engage employees and cater for their individual needs.

Aside from this, it is often the little things that make a big difference, such as calling employees by their name, asking them how they are, and taking mental note of the things that are important to them. And making time for them in your schedule. It sounds obvious I know, but many managers don't even make time for the people in their team.

And as well as all this obvious stuff, we can create the frameworks I mentioned above. And here is a really easy one that managers can deploy throughout their teams. It's called the Employee Confidence hub, and is the sweet spot between what the employee loves doing, what they are good at, and what the business needs. Finding this sweet spot requires the asking of three simple questions:

1. What do you love doing?

2. What are you good at?

3. What does the business need?

When your employee finds the one (or more) thing(s) that meet all the above three criteria, then you have an Employee Confidence hub. For example, let's say that Joe Bloggs loves creating new products and he is really good at locking himself away for hours and developing new software programs, and the business has a strategy to develop 10 new products a year. Set Joe Bloggs off on this path and he is going to make a big difference, and be brimming with confidence.

EMPLOYEE CONFIDENCE RULE 11 – LEVERAGING THE EMPLOYEE CONFIDENCE HUB (LIKE, GOOD, NEEDS)

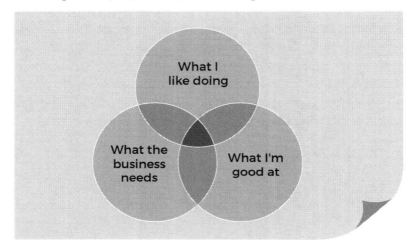

Achievements and contributions are recognised

When we think about Employee Engagement, we often think about all the nice things we need to provide for our employees to keep them happy at work and be excited about coming into work. I'm talking about free food, the on-site crèche and gym, getting to take a day off on your birthday, and all that nice stuff. All of this is great, and important, but means a one size fits all approach to your employees, and possibly you are wasting a lot of money on things which aren't necessarily important to everyone. It also addresses more of the basic human needs than the deeper psychological ones, like Maslow's self-actualisation need.

What is really important to everyone, regardless of their individual personality, is being recognised and rewarded for our individual and team contributions. Some of us need this external approval less than others, but when we receive it, it makes all of us feel good, even if it is just to confirm what we already knew inside. Let's look at how this might work in practice.

Many companies have reward programmes, like employee of the month, or a chairman's award, where employees are rewarded for specific, desired behaviours. These are great and often provide extended periods of motivation around a specific programme or initiative, like a wellbeing programme. I would suggest, however, that your managers go back to basics with rewards and recognition and build time into their schedule to offer that personal touch, and to actively seek out positive behaviours.

In one company I worked with, most employees were engineers or technically-minded individuals who had spent many years in an environment where they were expected to point out the failings in approaches and ideas. This was an extremely important behaviour in the interests of Quality and getting things right. What we discovered, however, was that this had become a default setting and managers were only noticing what their teams were doing wrong and going to great pains to point this out. As you can imagine, this was having a big impact on Employee Confidence.

In this story above, managers were trained and encouraged to start producing daily lists on their teams, where they gave equal weighting to what employees were doing right and what they were doing wrong, and every day the good behaviours were publicly reported and recognised. Employee Confidence improved drastically and so did productivity.

Performance beyond expectations is rewarded

So this is everyday performance, but what about when employees go the extra mile, which many do and often with little thanks or recognition? Well in our Employee Confidence hub above, we talked about Joe Bloggs really making a difference when we hit the sweet spot between what he loves doing, what he is good at, and what the business needs. But what is important now is how we recognise and reward this because this will keep him motivated for the long term and boost his personal growth and productivity.

In my experience, the Joe Bloggs situation does exist, even though it may seem rare. In fact, this type of employee often emerges by accident, but the problem is, no one recognises it, and soon he or she falters because of this lack of recognition and reward. What he needs is a personal potential plan[15] that documents and formalises this type of behaviour, and offers recognition, rewards, pay upgrades and even promotion. Mind you, not everyone is motivated by all of this so it's worth speaking to Joe, starting with the following statement:

"We love what you are doing. It's clear you are doing what you love and what you are good at, and that it's what the business needs."

And then going in with a powerful question:

"So, Joe, what would it take to get you to do more of this? What would keep you motivated?"

We need to build more of these types of questions into employee conversations, whether that be formal appraisals or even regular informal conversations, so that employees feel valued.

Employees Feel Listened To

Asking employees great questions is the first step in listening to our employees, and listening to our employees is another important part of that honest working environment we talked about earlier. And notice that the question above was an open one, starting with the word what: "…what would it take…?"

---

15   Personal potential plan – a plan an employee designs for themselves to help them define and reach their full potential

Whenever you ask an open question rather than a closed one, people are forced to think rather than give a simple yes/no answer which requires no thought power whatsoever. This means that asking an open question, starting with a what or a how, or even a what if, is a great way to start listening to your employees. When you encourage your employees to think, you are effectively asking them what they think, and they start to feel valued. Even a simple "What do you think?" is a great default question to have up your sleeve. There are four ways we can listen to our employees better:

Conduct regular surveys

We can do the coaching type of conversation just discussed, which happens on an individual and informal basis, and we can do a formal annual survey across the whole organisation, asking employees what they think. For employees to feel listened to here, what is important is the confidential nature of the survey. When individuals and teams cannot be identified and they feel able to tell you what they think, they will!

When it comes to valuing employees by listening to them, asking them what they think is a good start but it's not enough. Equally as important is to get an independent third party to analyse the survey results so that they are independent and therefore credible. We also need to develop, publish and get buy-in to a plan to address the identified improvements.

I once ran a Health and Safety survey within a large corporate, measuring Health and Safety culture, and hence the success of the associated culture change programme. The survey was anonymous and confidential. Employees responded to the survey in their thousands and were very keen to hear the results, reported on by an independent party. One year, full survey reports were provided to all regions, and workshops run with regional leadership teams to help them put together their three-year plans for Health and

Safety culture improvements based on their regional survey results. This showed employees that their survey responses had been really listened to.

Give everyone a voice

An Employee Engagement survey gives everyone a voice and this is very important if we want to value our employees. Sometimes, however, we fail to give certain populations within our companies a voice simply because we don't even give them a 'seat at the table' – a term used by Sheryl Sandberg in her book *Lean in*. An example of this is a company I used to work with where women were in the minority and nowhere was this more acute than in the boardroom. Hardly any management meetings had female representation. This not only affected the way the company was run and decisions were made but also the way the small population of women was represented within the company.

We all know that getting more women in the boardroom is a big issue today, but the issue goes far wider. It's less a gender issue and more a listening issue. Across our organisations, we need to look at what types of people we have, how we represent them, and how we give them a voice. In this respect, Employee Engagement is like marketing. If we were doing external consumer marketing, we would be breaking our audience down and profiling the different types of people we have in our organisation. But do we really do this within the internal communications department? Or are we treating our employee population more as one homogenous unit?

Ensure input from all

Let's assume that on a day-to-day basis we have an accurate representation of the organisation at meetings i.e. everyone has a seat at the table. Having a seat, however, is not enough because how often do we really listen to everyone at the table in a meeting? I can think of many meetings I have attended where it is dominated by just a few voices, and the meeting is ended and closed without further thought to the matter. In my experience, this problem falls into two categories:

1. The person that doesn't speak at all

2. The person that speaks and isn't listened to

As an example of this, I was working with a technology company and we had weekly management meetings to get an update on where we were with the launch of the new software products and input from all business areas. The issue was that we had both category 1 and category 2 problems in there.

The person in category 1 said practically nothing all through the meeting and we never knew what he was thinking, being forced to read body language and minute facial gestures to know what was going on. The person in category 2, however, always had plenty to say, but because of a prior bad experience when he had not given us the true picture around a previous software product, any intervention by him was received with nods and yeses, but I am pretty sure no one was really listening.

So my question to you is this. If you have problem category 1 and 2 in your meetings, how do you know you are getting all the input you need for your business for starters, and from an engagement point of view, as neither of these employees are being listened to, or feeling valued?

Tell employees how their ideas have been used

We all know that communication is a two-way process, like a simple sender-receiver model for the telephone, but how often do we remember this? Most of us are in send or transmit mode only, or in receive mode only, and sometimes both at the same time but without any room for listening or feedback loops.

If we want to listen actively to our employees, to make them feel valued, we need to not just listen to them but to show them they've been understood. We can do this in a number of ways, and feedback to employees can be immediate or delayed, depending on how much information analysis is required for the feedback to be formulated.

Let's say we get our employees involved in improving safety culture at the workplace, and they come up with a whole host of ideas to present to management, through their worker-led network and associated committee. When these employees have worked hard to do the right thing, they want to know the impact of their hard work. One way to do this, and one I have seen work very well in practice, is to install poster boards on workers' sites which show a visual map of progress of continuous improvement ideas. This means employees can see their progress and are likely to continue with their hard work.

Employees are Encouraged

All employees, regardless of professional achievements, skills or status in the organisation, need encouragement and support. They also need a good coach, and to be able to coach themselves, asking themselves the right questions and holding a positive and supportive voice inside their heads. And we can encourage our employees in three key ways:

Have personal as well as business goals

Many companies have personal development plans for their employees, and these plans come from training needs identified in performance appraisal campaigns, and linked to future personal objectives linked to wider company objectives. But how personal do these development plans really go? Are the training and development needs identified between manager and employee enough to get the employee engaged and confident?

In the previous section I discussed the proposed Employee Confidence hub, where the stuff an employee loves doing and is good at coincides neatly with what the business or the department needs. This brings great alignment between employee and company and gives both parties confidence in the direction they are following. What if we were to think outside the box on Engagement and give our employees a really good reason to stay with the company in the long term, and feel supremely confident?

What if we were to put an extra line item in the personal development plan that allowed the employee to write down a personal goal that had absolutely nothing to do with the business? Now you might think this is going a bit too far since the employee is there to do a job and to focus purely on the business. Why would we want our employees spending time on anything that wasn't work related?

When you do something genuine for someone, for nothing, or give them something for free, then rather than put you at a disadvantage, it encourages that person to give more of themselves and do something for you. It's called the Law of Reciprocity, detailed in Cialdini's great book *Influence*. You are probably already doing this with other offerings in your Engagement portfolio, but what if you were to support all employees to set one personal goal each, and then see the impact that it has on their engagement, confidence and the business? Very often there is an overlap which can be linked back into the employee's job, and at the very least, it boosts morale and confidence.

Support goal achievement

And what if you were to go one step further and encourage employees not just to think about setting a personal goal and noting it on an additional personal potential plan but also support them to help them realise that goal? I know that again this is outside the company's professional scope, but it doesn't have to take long, and imagine how encouraged your employees would feel!

If you want the wow factor for your Employee Engagement plans, the potential to impress your human capital goes far beyond the short-term satisfaction offered by free food, gyms, bonuses and crèches. Helping your people to achieve their own personal goals is Employee Engagement on steroids!

When each employee comes up with their own personal goal, and it is submitted to Human Resources as part of their personal development plan, you set up an automated system which sends them an email congratulating them on setting their personal goal and giving them a graphic which says the following:

It is (insert date) and I am/have (insert specific, measurable goal). To do this, I need to ask myself these three questions every day:

1. Why do I want to achieve this goal? What will this goal give me?

2. What action have I taken towards this goal today?

3. Who will hold me accountable for the achievement of this goal?

Then simply ask the employee to take a photo of the graphic and save it as the screensaver on their mobile phone. And it works. It works because goals require three things to come to fruition:

1. Motivation – this comes from remembering their why.

2. Commitment – which comes from taking action (even if only small) towards the goal every day.

3. Accountability – having that one person who is going to keep asking you how you are getting on with your goal and what is stopping you from taking the action required to achieve it.

In summary, SMART goals are effective, but MCA goals – goals with Motivation, Commitment and Accountability – will greatly increase the probability of that goal being achieved!

EMPLOYEE CONFIDENCE RULE 12 – THE MCA OF GOAL ACHIEVEMENT

M – MOTIVATION
(your why)

C – COMMITMENT
(the strength of your why)

A – ACCOUNTABILITY
(finding others to keep you on track)

Assign 'stretch' activities

If we want our employees to be leaders, they need to grow, personally. And if we want them to grow, we need to give them what I would call 'stretch' activities. Stretch activities are work which allows us to further develop existing skills or to develop new skills. Doing so will be a function of the skillset we are focusing on, which we could call capability, and the area in which we apply it.

As an example, I once trained some coaches in conversational change techniques to work in an office environment, enabling them to create an excellent culture for leadership in the context of Quality.

Now what if we were to take those same coaches, once experienced, and offer them the opportunity to take their skills out on to more operational and complex worksites, where their communication skills would really be tested? I'm thinking of construction or complex manufacturing sites, or even cargo and transportation vessels. This would definitely be a stretch activity and the coaches would learn a great deal from this.

If you want to stretch your employees, why not create an additional section on their personal development plan for this? You may already note down their training needs, based on an identified business need, but if you assess and deploy stretch activities you get several benefits as follows:

1. The employee grows and develops – benefiting them and the business.

2. The stretch area benefits.

3. The business gets additional employees with experience and/or skills across several different areas – extremely useful in times when resources are tight.

And to make it easier to assess possibilities for stretch activities, simply use the 2 x 2 matrix in diagram 3 below. Where existing capabilities are applied to new areas of the business or vice versa, there is stretch involved, and where new capabilities are applied to a new area of the business, the stretch is extreme. Extreme isn't impossible but it is important to put a safety net in place here, possibly by assigning a coach or mentor to the employee subject to the extreme stretch activity. If not, that high potential employee could soon go into overwhelm.

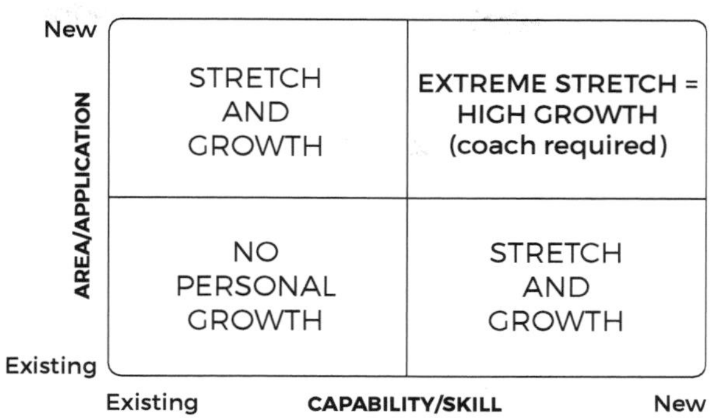

Diagram 3

EMPLOYEE CONFIDENCE RULE 13 – EMPLOYEE CONFIDENCE THROUGH STRETCH

EXISTING CAPABILITY + EXISTING AREA =
NO PERSONAL GROWTH

EXISTIING CAPABIITY + NEW AREA = STRETCH

NEW CAPABILITY + EXISTING AREA = STRETCH

NEW CAPABILITY + NEW AREA =
EXTREME STRETCH =
HIGH GROWTH (COACH REQUIRED)

Employees are Supported

We are working towards an honest working environment where our employees are valued, listened to and encouraged. We also need them to be supported, in all areas, and especially if we want them to take the personal risk required with stretch activities. If we want our people to be leaders and adopt new behaviours, we also need to support them to do so and make it easy for them to behave and grow in the direction we want.

Leadership behaviours are recognised and rewarded

Many employees are already self-starters and that's presumably why they were hired – because they are talented and take the initiative. So why do we need to support them? Aren't they already doing just fine on their own? Well, let me give you an example.

When I worked with a company with technical and complex worksites, we developed and implemented a behavioural change programme, including training coaches for the worksites themselves. We asked for one key leadership behaviour – Intervention. What was meant by this was that everyone in the company was empowered, and even expected, to intervene, speak up, and stop the job taking place if they perceived there to be a potential incident that might impact business results or company reputation.

This behaviour was requested and supported right from the top of the organisation, by the CEO, and many workers started to intervene. Some, however, did not, and this was backed up by the results of a survey, suggesting that a small but still significant percentage of employees still didn't feel empowered to intervene. So what was going wrong exactly? The behaviour was backed by the CEO, so how much more empowerment did they need?

What I think was happening was that the message wasn't filtering down correctly to lower levels of management, and to clients and key partners on the worksites, and attempts to intervene and make highly costly stops to work activities were being met with resistance. In a nutshell, if we want employees to adopt certain leadership behaviours, we need to address more than the behaviours themselves. We also need a system in place to ensure the behaviours are welcomed, praised, recognised and even rewarded by managers.

Line managers promote employees upwards

While we are on the topic of supporting our employees, think about the best boss you ever had. What was it about that boss that you liked? What specifically did he or she do that you particularly admired? I have had several bosses in my lifetime that I have particularly admired and one key trait comes to mind. That is a boss's ability to 'have your back', to trust in your skills, abilities and decisions, and to back you when times get tough.

Some years ago, I was working as a lecturer in a business school and had only been teaching for a year when two of my students questioned the marks I gave them on one of their papers. They took the matter to my boss and I was expecting to be in trouble. My boss, however, gave the students this as a response: "The young lady you are complaining about is one of the best lecturers we have ever had, and if I hear another word on the matter, your marks will be reduced further!" I remember these words to this day, I felt so supported and valued.

What if you had a boss who didn't just support you like this but also promoted your thoughts and ideas, making sure your achievements are visible to senior management? Did you ever have a boss who did that for you? Are you a boss who does that for your people? I firmly believe that the best bosses are all about their people rather than themselves, and this inspires employees and instils them with a lot of confidence.

Line managers are interested in what their teams do

Let's keep thinking about that one boss we admire, or admired, and where that admiration came from. Now we all know that people at that level don't have much time for 'doing' and operate at the big picture level with a wide overarching knowledge of everything going on in the company. At the same time, it is hugely empowering, engaging and confidence boosting for an employee for someone at that high level to show an interest in what they do. It is human nature to want to feel important, and when someone shows an interest in what we do, we feel important.

I remember one manager who always had time for me and asked me great questions that made me think – about how and why I do what I do. Through these conversations alone I felt engaged, empowered and confident, and then one day I saw him stand up and speak at a management meeting. The discussion had got on to culture change and the guy stood up and spoke out as a strong and knowledgeable advocate for our programme. I couldn't have done it better myself, and felt extremely supported.

CHAPTER 5

Today's employees need more than Engagement

Today's employees have more opportunities, more choices and more information than ever before, and reduced attention spans. There has been a surge in individualisation and personalisation, and there are too many competing messages that aren't relevant enough. For all these reasons, today's Employee Engagement model is struggling to make an impact. Employee Confidence is the missing link because it encourages employees to overcome their fears and not only engage but become leaders, in an environment that supports personal risk taking and enables critical conversations[16] to happen. With confidence, engagement has more chance of success because without it engagement is stifled, and with it the already engaged are boosted and the disengaged converted.

---

16   Critical Conversations – conversations that need to take place and for which a positive outcome is critical, due to their influence on strategic compliance issues such as Health, Safety, Quality, Ethics etc.

Today's employees want to feel engaged at work, and companies need to have them engaged, but how to do it is complex and the context equally so. When we do it right, however, we have an opportunity to move into the sphere of Employee Confidence, creating a leadership movement that not only leads to culture change but is culture change itself. Let's look at some of the reasons why old Engagement models may not be working and why we might want to embrace a different and more beneficial approach.

Today's Employees are Different From Yesterday's

The world has changed a great deal over the last few decades, meaning that employees have had to adapt and change to the new world and circumstances they live in. Furthermore, the sheer pace of change is now exponential, spurred on by technological changes that are taking us into a new era. Today's employees are living in a different world and this has led to different needs and aspirations. And the question is, has our model for Employee Engagement kept up? Before we answer it, let's look at four ways in which today's employees are different:

They have more opportunities and more choice

With the advent of the internet and mobile phones, today's employees now have access to more information than ever before, and across more channels. We are firmly in the information age, where knowledge is power and experts are emerging all over the place. Anywhere you can find a niche, you will find an expert, and information and expertise are being repackaged, recreated and further segmented, with niches emerging all the time. Never have employees had such a wide-ranging opportunity for their own personal development, and they are taking it. They also want flexibility in their lifestyles and know they don't have to depend on an employer for this.

At business networking events, we see an emergence of people talking of a 'portfolio' business or lifestyle, where they combine several different jobs into one week, doing one thing one day and another the next, on a freelance or self-employed basis. This may well be a win-win for both employee and company, where both get the flexibility they require, but let's think about the implications. Does this model improve or reduce Employee Engagement?

It all depends whether the company considers a contractor as an employee, and if it does, the employee could be more engaged because their needs around flexible working are being met. If the company favours permanent employees, however, it may start to struggle to keep them, and there may also be a change in the power balance between them and their employees. The latter don't need that stable corporate job for life they thought they did, and with all the niching happening, companies may find skills in short supply.

Information overload is reducing attention spans

The downside of all this information coming our way is information overload and it's reducing our attention spans. According to Mihaly Csikszentmihalyi, the Hungarian psychologist, in his book *Flow*, our human brains are only able to process about 126 bits of information per second out of the potentially millions of bits of information we have available to us in that same second. Our brains, then, act as a giant sieve, filtering out information according to where we place our attention.

Having vast amounts of information available to us, and at our fingertips, via our smartphones and other technological devices, is all very well but it's challenging our attention spans. Even when focused on work, then, our employees are struggling to focus on it. And that's just the information overload in the workplace, with all the emails and phone calls coming in, but what if we add all our personal stuff into the mix?

The marketing industry has the same problem. How do they get our attention to sell us their products? How many times do they need to get their messages in front of us before we take it in, and act on it, through an enquiry or even a purchase? Employers have the same problem, although they may not be quite as aware of it. And how can they engage employees when they don't even have their attention?

In my experience, employees often do believe in and buy into corporate programmes and initiatives, but they are suffering from corporate initiative overload and need help to understand them. Employee bandwidth is far slimmer than before, and to connect with it, in a meaningful way, we need to think differently. One solution is to develop shared content and run joint sessions. This keeps the strain on employee bandwidth to a minimum and ensures both messages get through.

Aspirations are higher than before

Today's employees have higher aspirations than before. They want more for themselves in the workplace, and they are creating their career the way they want it. We have a growing number of women or 'mumpreneurs' – women who have started their own businesses out of necessity, having had a baby and then discovered on going back to work that they couldn't work with the flexibility they needed to be a good mum. Many decided then to leave their corporate employer and set up their own business, networking and collaborating locally with other mums doing the same thing. Some discover their passion and great success, and they become entrepreneurs. This boosts their confidence and they discover that they want more from life, and can get more. The corporates have no chance of getting them back.

And this may be true of the population in general, because it's not just women that want flexible work – men want it too. The

Uber and Deliveroo phenomenon has been due in part to their drivers relishing the flexible work patterns they were offered, and reflects the biggest change in work patterns since the industrial revolution, known as the gig economy[17]. Not only have workers managed to secure the flexibility they require, taking on only the work they want, when they want, and with who they want, but are also sometimes able to secure the same rights as employees.

Customisation is key

Every employee is unique, so why do our Employee Engagement strategies treat all employees as one homogenous unit? With more information available to us, in more segmented chunks and across different channels, our thirst for customised products and services is being fuelled. We expect it from our consumer products and services, and need it in our workplaces. We are all on information overload, particularly from email, and want to be able to access only the information we need, when we need it. We don't want to waste time on stuff that detracts from what is important.

One organisation I know approaches this dilemma through a digital self-service hub for employees. This hub allows employees access to basic information products online, but with a multitude of ways in which the employee can use and engage with them. It recognises that everyone has different engagement styles, depending on their working and communication preferences, and that engagement needs to be addressed through many different channels and applications. When these options exist, employees feel special and important, and engagement and confidence grows. Companies that recognise this fact are leveraging technology to make their offerings more tailored to the individual customer, and more individual, but are we extending the same service to our employees?

---

17   An environment where temporary contracts are common and organisations pay workers accordingly for short-term engagements or 'gigs'

The Current Engagement Model Isn't Working

So, we know that the current engagement model isn't working for everyone, and when we consider all the variables in today's working environment, it is clear why. Not only has the existing Employee Engagement model not evolved with the changing working environment, but there are also several other challenges to consider, and let's look at three of them here:

Too many competing messages

For starters, there are too many competing messages, and we alluded to this in the section on information overload above. Never have we employees been so bombarded with requests for our attention, and when it comes to Employee Engagement, for our hearts and minds. Engagement, however, is optional, so if the many messages we get start to compete, we get confused and simply ignore all of them.

Of course, one solution is to reduce the confusion by joining forces with other campaigns and programmes within the company, competing with us for employee bandwidth, and look at where we can collaborate and share airtime, as discussed earlier. Your other option is simply to stand out more, and this might be easier than you think. In the race for hearts and minds, most of us are looking to the next technological development, like the digital hub described above, and hoping our employees will be impressed by our gizmos and gadgets. This may be worth a shot, of course, but there are cheaper and more effective options.

I once worked with a company where each division was effectively competing to recruit trainers for their programme. Not only that, but these potential trainers were highly skilled, from an operational point of view, and much in demand from other areas of the business. So how did they engage these trainers? Well one division decided to go for the personal touch, creating a gift for all those who were certified to deliver the new programme. Another went back to basics and wrote personal, handwritten letters to all potential recruits, explaining why they had been chosen to be involved. Both strategies cut through the competing messages to reach their target.

Messages aren't personal or individual enough

The personal touch is important, and sometimes it's not just about reaching out in a personal way to someone, as described above. The above strategies work but they tend to only have short-term impact. The recipient of the gift or the letter might feel important for a few weeks, but then there will be some other programme or initiative vying for their time. This means we need to work harder to get a personal or individual message across.

The only way to engage employees in the long term is to address everyone's personal motivation for getting involved. You need to appeal to what's deeply important to that person and structure your message in those terms.

In one company I worked with, they came up with an excellent way of engaging workers on a project out in Africa, encouraging every single one of them to get involved and look out for each other, to stay safe. How they did it was very clever. They started from the idea that family is the key driver of behaviour for people across the globe, and named the campaign after a common male name in that part of the world. Since the workforce was predominantly male, and everyone knew someone called the name chosen, everyone could relate to it and got involved.

Not everyone wants to be a leader

Often when we seek engagement from our employees, we want them to get involved in something, to do something, to take some action, or adopt some specific behaviour. Nearly always, what we are looking for is for our employees to behave as leaders. But does everyone really want to be a leader?

There are many models of leadership, with transformational leadership being the most relevant to culture change, as discussed earlier. This model of leadership starts with the individual themselves, and their own level of self-awareness, and my interpretation is that it asks for essentially three things:

1. Being ethical and a role model that others aspire to follow (Charisma)

2. Caring about others and paying them individual attention (Caring)

3. Speaking out in support of the ethics in point 1 above (Calling out)

EMPLOYEE CONFIDENCE RULE 14
THE 3 CS OF CULTURE CHANGE LEADERSHIP

CHARISMA -
Being an ethical role model that others aspire to follow

CARING -
Caring about others and paying them individual attention

CALLING OUT -
Speaking out in support of the ethics in
point 1 above

Many of our employees would easily follow the first two points, but the sticking point is often on point 3, when they are required to speak out.

I worked with a technology company once where the majority were technical people, with an introverted personality preference. Of course, they had strong ethical values and cared about people but they weren't keen to speak out. When employees operate from an introversion preference, they may shy away from confrontation, preferring to stay in the background.

So not everyone wants to be a leader. And if we want to convince them, we need to give them confidence, and give them the skills and training they need. In a company I worked with on a safety culture programme, this problem was recognised, and a one-day training course was developed to help people have what they perceived to be difficult conversations (the speaking out), by pitching them as 'critical' i.e. must have, conversations, and giving a simple process for doing so. The skills may have been alien to them at first, but when taught in a process type way, the technical employees engaged with it quickly.

Employee Confidence is the Missing Link

When employees are taught leadership skills in the right way, and in a language that resonates with them, their confidence will start to grow. For some people, a lot of confidence is required because there are not just personality barriers but cultural barriers as well. Hofstede's work on culture suggests that where countries have a high power-distance ratio, the culture is hierarchical and it is not usual to confront or question someone higher up than you. Confidence is required to overcome these barriers because:

Confidence encourages introverts to become leaders

When confidence is present, it encourages introverts to become change leaders, where speaking out is a necessity. For those favouring introvert behaviours, speaking out directly may take them out of their comfort zone, or there may simply not be enough belief for someone to feel confident enough to do so. Confidence comes from excellence in communication, and excellent communicators have flexibility – the ability to delve deep into a fantastic toolbox of communication tools and find the right tool for the situation. One such tool is stories and metaphors, and it's a great way to help introverts speak out and become extroverts when they need to be. Stories have the power to convey a message in a non-confrontational way.

Many years ago, I lost my best friend from my school days. She was only 21 and was killed in a car accident. She was the only one in the car not wearing a seatbelt, and when the car crashed she was thrown out of the car and killed instantly. If someone had spoken out that day and refused to let her travel in the car without a seatbelt, things might have been very different. This is a true story and I tell it every time someone tries to travel in a car with me without wearing a seatbelt. It has impact because it is emotional and everyone can relate to it. It instantly motivates others to put on their seatbelt and it gives me confidence go into battle for 'the right thing' without being misunderstood. Without the story to hand, I may stay silent instead of speaking out.

Confidence creates the environment for personal risk taking

Employee Confidence creates an environment for personal risk taking. I have heard some people call it psychological risk. What is the risk? Whether introvert or extrovert, we are all hard wired to connect with people and our biggest fear is breaking the relationship. In her book entitled *The Female Brain*, Dr Louann Brizendine suggests that women's brains are designed to seek connections with people. Could it be then that preserving the relationship is critical to human relations? And when I say preserve the relationship, I mean not doing or saying anything that might offend the other person or cause them to dislike us or think badly of us. Worrying about this is fear of any difficult conversation upsetting a relationship, and I don't believe this is purely a female concern either.

I firmly believe that this fear, and the risk, can be eliminated when we create the right environment for personal risk taking. One example of how to do this in the workplace is to focus your culture change programme as much on teaching the skills for receiving intervention as on the skills for making the actual intervention itself. In my experience, this focus is always missing in companies, and can be resolved with a global communications campaign to encourage people to accept intervention, welcome it and praise the person making it.

Confidence comes from a coaching culture

When we create the environment for personal risk taking, what we do effectively is to create a safe space for fears to be stepped into and overcome – those fears at the root of confidence. We create the safety net that allows us to take a risk, without psychological damage to ourselves or others. When we cater for any possible fears that might come up, then there is no reason why all employees can't be confident and become leaders for any strategic issue of the company's choosing.

Another way of creating that safety net is to build coaching skills as well as leadership skills. In fact, coaching is just transformational leadership in action, so when we build coaching skills in our teams, we are creating not just leaders but transformational leaders. Transformational leaders bring about change, as we mentioned earlier.

Imagine the scenario where you have a group of workers on a dangerous worksite, with complex machinery and structures to be dismantled from one site and then reassembled somewhere else. The workers are under extreme time pressure and face a hazardous environment full of risk to their health and wellbeing. Why not have health and wellbeing buddies deployed as part of the workforce, but purely in a coaching role, providing that safety net? As Jiminy Cricket was to Pinocchio, they act as the workers' conscience, asking the right questions, in the right way, and at the right time, to encourage them to work in a way that promotes health and wellbeing.

Confidence leads to critical conversations

There are many examples of difficult conversations in the workplace: telling a worker they are not doing a very good job or there has been a complaint against them, or even that their position is being made redundant. To be able to conduct such a conversation, face to face, with minimal psychological damage, takes skill. In fact, it takes leadership. But what if the conversation is something even more serious than that e.g. on a safety, health, or ethical issue, like bullying or harassment?

When the stakes are high for these difficult conversations, they become critical conversations. In the above examples, where the conversations are difficult, some people choose to delegate them to others, or to not have the conversation at all, preferring a phone call or even an email. It takes real confidence to have difficult conversations, and leadership to have critical conversations.

One such critical conversation could be employees in a finance department spotting a problem with a payment procedure. They are concerned that payment details could have been compromised, but here's the dilemma. If they speak out and stop the payment, the whole project will be delayed and it could be very costly. The client won't be happy and their credibility might even come into question. And even worse, it might turn out to be a false alarm. But the risk is clear, and speaking out is the right thing to do. With confidence, employees will do it because they know their values and are prepared to act on them.

With Confidence, Engagement Has More Chance of Success

Confidence is not separate from engagement – it boosts it. Employees will engage without confidence, but how far will that engagement go? Will it go as far as personal responsibility and action? Some action may be taken, but what about when it really counts and requires personal responsibility, like the IT security example described above? With confidence, engagement has more chance of success, and for three main reasons:

A lack of confidence can stifle engagement

A lack of confidence can stifle engagement because your employees won't feel able to lead culture change. I remember when I was working as a coach within a construction company and coaching site workers around intervention for safety. One girl I worked with said to me, "I don't feel able to intervene and stop the job." When I asked her why, she said, "Because I don't have the authority. No one listens to me." And then I said to her, "If you did have the authority, what would you do?" and she replied, "I'd go up there and show them the accident that's waiting to happen."

When we look at all the engagement figures, or rather the lack of, let's not assume that our employees just aren't interested in what we want them to do. I am sure that many of them are interested but need a bit of a helping hand to step over the threshold from engagement to confidence.

What I then said to her was, "How much authority do you need to point out what someone neutral with an independent eye can see far more clearly than someone too busy doing the job has overlooked?"

She looked at me and said, "None, I guess."

All I did was bring a sense of reality to her perception of the problem by suggesting how a neutral and logical bystander might see the situation, giving her the confidence to move beyond her self-created barriers.

Confidence boosts the 'already engaged'

Whilst a lack of confidence can stifle engagement, we can also see evidence that confidence can boost the engagement levels of those who are 'already engaged'. Have you ever heard the expression that you only really learn something when you have to teach it? There's nothing like the pressure of having to teach something to get you to make sure you really understand it.

And when you really understand something, you are much better at explaining that something to others. If it's something technical, you need to be able to understand it so well that you can break it down into something quite simple and convey its meaning in layman's terms, and possibly through metaphor and analogy. The same goes for engagement. You may have some employees in your company that are already engaged, but is there even more potential lurking in there?

Here is an example. When I ran a culture change training within a manufacturing company, we took the decision to use only in-house trainers and coaches for the programme. The only problem was the programme was mature, the content stale and the trainers were getting a bit bored. We decided to tempt them with new training and a new identity as coaches for conversational behavioural change at the worksites.

Not only did we achieve our objective but there was an additional by-product. What we noticed was that these people were not just engaged in the programme but they became active ambassadors for it, talking about it at all their regular meetings and recruiting others to get involved. We saw a similar outcome earlier with the recruitment of a network of volunteer trainers for a culture change programme.

Confidence converts the 'disengaged'

What about those employees in your company that are disengaged – the ones you need to bring on line? What is stopping them becoming engaged? Could it again be a lack of confidence? Not necessarily, but in my experience, whilst confidence may not necessarily be the root cause of all engagement issues, it is always a symptom of the problem.

With one company, for example, where no one was really interested in the environment, or in protecting it, a programme was launched to raise environmental awareness within the company, but it didn't really take off. Employees perceived management to be just paying lip service to the whole thing and left it to the environmental specialists. That was until someone had the idea of going out and asking workers what was stopping them from getting involved, and they started talking about not feeling confident enough to speak about environmental issues within the organisation because they didn't know enough about it.

Once employees knew more about the topic, and that environmental stuff wasn't just about recycling, it was also about protecting the local wildlife, for example, they signed up in their hundreds. Here increased awareness had led to increased confidence which led to increased levels of engagement and leadership.

CHAPTER 6

Today's companies need confident change leaders

Traditionally leadership resides at the top of an organisation, where management style is autocratic and transactional, and information only travels one way – downwards. As a result, employees comply and rarely perform beyond expectations. When we push leadership downwards, however, this self-service model reduces central costs, and creates an empowered workforce that becomes much more autonomous and productive. Leadership means everyone taking personal responsibility for addressing non-compliance, and this only happens when employees want to make a difference, believe they can make a difference, and know they can. Transformational rather than transactional leadership is the secret, aligning everyone around a cause and setting an example that others aspire to follow.

When companies reach a certain size, they change the way they operate, to be more efficient and more effective with a larger number of employees. There is a recognition that senior managers cannot do everything, and that certain things need to be delegated out to managers of managers, to middle managers, and to front-line workers. One of these elements is leadership. The larger a company gets, the more it needs its employees to step up and show leadership. Leadership, however, requires engagement, and engagement is more likely to lead to leadership when confidence exists.

Traditional Leadership Happens at the Top of the Organisation

When you hear the word leadership, though, what do you think of? I think many of us would think of an activity performed by someone with status and authority within an organisation – someone in a position of power, required to lead others. The top of an organisation is the most obvious place for leadership to exist. But what does this mean for Employee Engagement and our new aspirations for Employee Confidence?

Its style is transactional and autocratic

Where leadership exists with position power, it can sometimes be rather autocratic, with the people at the top of the organisation, or in a managerial role, telling others very directly what they want them to do. If you have ever worked for this kind of manager, there are advantages and disadvantages: on the one hand, it's clear what is required of you, but on the other hand, it doesn't do wonders for your drive or creativity. Of course, there is a time and a place for this type of leadership, especially in critical situations when there is no time to debate how and why things need to be done, but there is another, more powerful option. It all depends what you want to achieve.

I saw one example of this type of leadership, and it came from the top of the organisation. Employees were told in no uncertain terms what to do, how to do it and when, and in language that made it clear that non-compliance was not an option. Under this type of regime, even the most confident type of employee starts to comply and loses confidence along the way. Especially if in this case they start to challenge and question the orders, and are not listened to. This type of interaction chips away at the confidence of your employees. They question their right to think, their opinions, and their abilities, particularly their leadership abilities.

Information flow is one way

In the above example, information moves very clearly downwards, with less room for information to move upwards. Of course, all the mechanisms are there, but employees start to fear speaking out. The type of autocratic leadership behaviour described above stops employees speaking out because the senior manager has created an environment of compliance. Your employees become your 'yes' men and women, and the only information you get moving upwards is that word 'yes'.

I experienced this type of environment when working as a consultant. Against a backdrop of dramatic change due to an organisational restructure, pressure grew for senior management to perform and deliver results. At the same time, some staff were being made redundant, due to the restructure, and this was compounding the pressure. The company was already like a pressure cooker, and information was moving down the company, in direct and unequivocal fashion. With no room and no space to question anything, Employee Confidence started to wane and employee communication went underground.

Pockets of worker communication started to develop in work areas, where workers complained and gossiped about their situation, over coffee, lunch or the printing machine. With no official outlet for this kind of communication, it swirled around dangerously like a poisonous mist, contaminating any confidence and creativity that still existed. Human beings are born to communicate and to express their views. When we don't allow them to communicate upwards, it's going to affect not only Employee Engagement but also Employee Confidence.

Employees comply, and perform only to expectations

In the example above, I talked about employees becoming your 'yes' people. On the face of it, it sounds great! Isn't that every employer's dream to have employees who do exactly what is expected of them? Of course, sometimes, yes! No one wants employees who don't follow instructions and break the rules. Or do they? It all depends on the context. Sometimes extraordinary situations emerge that are unpredictable, and in these kinds of situations, like an accident or emergency for example, you may need your people to follow the rules but also to think outside of the box sometimes as well.

And it's not just emergency or unusual situations where we need our people to think outside the box. With the extreme rate of change happening in the world today, we rely on our employees to come up with the innovative solutions that will get us ahead in the marketplace. Some companies have known this for a long time, and create an environment where their employees can create and innovate constantly, but others are slow to do the same.

So sometimes we need employees to break the rules, and sometimes we need employees to tell us where we are going wrong and/or could do things differently. We need to harness the collective brainpower of everyone in our companies, not just the brainpower of a few at the top of an organisation that go unchallenged. Otherwise, this becomes 'groupthink', where one person with more position power subtly influences the entire group, and could lead to erroneous and costly decisions.

There is also another reason why we might not want employees to simply comply, and a story a friend told me illustrates this perfectly. He told me that some years before we worked together, he was a young and ambitious manager working in the retail sector. He led in the autocratic, transactional style described above, and cut his staff very little slack. He even remembers his workers asking for the radio on in the warehouse and he refused to allow it, encouraging them to focus on their work instead.

This style served him well, that was until one day a massive shipment of goods arrived and he asked his workers to work an additional night shift to get all the new goods unloaded and stored away. It wasn't part of the workers' contracts and they didn't have to do it. With no goodwill or confidence created previously by the manager, the workers refused to work the overtime and the result was pure compliance instead of the required 'extra mile' in an unusual situation.

Leadership For All Has Many Benefits

Over the last few decades we have seen a growing number of organisations leverage the internet to reduce costs, creating a self-service model for those areas of their operation where technology allows customers to do a stage of the process themselves. The airline industry is a good example, where customers are asked to print their own boarding passes before they fly, saving airlines one step in the process and the printing cost.

The internet in general is also being used for wider self-service activities like online shopping, where a whole section of the sales and fulfilment process is taken online. And there are many more examples of this 'self-service' model, originally coined from self-service canteens and restaurants, where the part of the process that involved the food moving from kitchen to customer table was delegated to the customers themselves. There are three main advantages to extending leadership to the rest of the organisation:

A self-service model reduces central costs

A self-service model reduces costs for the organisation – the cost of servicing a customer. But what if we deploy it to employees? If it reduces central costs to the organisation, then why not get employees to take on more of the workload? The same goes for leadership: why leave it at the top of the organisation when pushing it downwards would allow employees to take on more of the responsibility?

When employees take on more leadership responsibility, it doesn't necessarily reduce costs of leadership training, since a certain amount is required at all levels and it may not be the same kind of leadership we are looking at anyway. But when leadership occurs at the bottom of the organisation, and is led by workers, then it is the resulting impact that reduces central costs. Let me explain.

In a previous project I worked on, leadership was promoted at the bottom of the organisation, in the context of worker safety on sites with complex equipment and machinery. Leadership was encouraged through a peer-to-peer observation system, where employees were trained to go out and conduct peer-to-peer observations around safe and unsafe behaviours, and use the information gleaned to improve worker engagement around safety and implement practical safety improvements.

In this case, the workload for safety improvements, through leadership activity and behaviours, was clearly pushed down to the workers, enhancing the ownership and overall result, and reducing central costs. And the way it did this was not by making leadership any cheaper but by enhancing the value brought to the business from its investment in leadership skills training.

Employees feel more ownership and empowerment

Leadership activity conducted by the workers themselves, through worker-led improvement networks, and with a particular aim in mind, has other benefits. In fact, these benefits are probably far greater than the benefit of reducing central costs. One of these benefits for workers is a feeling of more ownership, which drives productivity, allowing real improvements in the area in question to be realised.

Let's use the example of the peer-to-peer observation system above, led by site workers, with the aim of making incremental improvements in safety and overall improvement in the safety culture on each site. Safety culture improves over time, as a company gets more mature in its approach. Where maturity is low, safety professionals may be viewed as 'safety police', there only to police the local safety rules and to sanction non-compliance. This kind of culture does not promote engagement.

Imagine a site with a more mature safety culture, where safety professionals are a friendly face, there to look out for people and help everyone stay safe. Safety is everyone's job and everyone gets involved. One day the manager speaks at the weekly meeting and sets all the workers a challenge. He or she suggests that the workers take on their own safety culture improvement project. They will have full ownership of it, observations conducted will be peer-to-peer only, and the system will be confidential, run by a self-selected committee. How engaged do you think the workers are now?

This is what I have seen happening with many operational sites, with massive improvements made in strategic issues such as

Safety, Quality, Security, Health, Environment, Ethics and so on, and mainly because it is led by the workers, who are given the leadership skills to succeed. Leadership at employee level really does have a massive impact on productivity, because of ownership and empowerment.

Employees make faster and better decisions

Sometimes leadership at local level is required every single day. Employees are required to make decisions, and quickly, because they work autonomously and in complex and high hazard environments. One such example might be a commercial ship, for example, where the potential for change is far greater. Even with the best will in the world, and the best planning and preparation, unforeseen changes can and do happen all the time, for unpredictable reasons such as weather. And when they do, the knock-on effect on the project schedule can be enormous. If everything is planned around a ship departing at a certain time, and weather delays it, then decisions must be made quickly, and the impact of those decisions communicated up and down the supply chain.

In this case, leadership at the bottom of the organisation becomes critical to decision making, and to minimising impact on the schedule. When the ship's crew have leadership skills, they think in a more reasoned manner under pressure and changing conditions, communicate effectively, and take personal responsibility to make sure the right things are done, in the right way, at the right time. When change has to be managed quickly, leadership skills are not only a nice to have, but mission critical, and to have to refer decisions back up the chain would be hugely counterproductive. They might also have an impact on other critical issues such as Health, Safety, Security and the Environment.

Leadership For All Requires Personal Responsibility

Leadership without position power requires personal responsibility, and this is important because it's a feeling – a feeling of being responsible for something – and the way we feel drives our behaviour. For personal responsibility, the behaviour the feeling drives is action. And as mentioned earlier, there can be many barriers to moving from across the threshold from feeling you should take action to actually taking action, so the feeling has to be a strong one. So how specifically does leadership create personal responsibility? I believe it does so in three ways, and these ways are aligned to the way our minds work and to our likelihood of becoming leaders. These three ways are as follows:

Employees want to make a difference

To show leadership and personal responsibility, the first thing that needs to happen is for us to want to make a difference. Without this 'wanting' there is no motivation to think or feel in a different way from what we do currently. Wanting to make a difference is about feeling passionate about something, because it reflects employees' personal values, and this is often steeped in past and emotional experiences, and what is important to them in the present. It can often also reflect a significant life event that has made them think differently i.e. having a family – an event that may change your personal values and priorities.

Let's take the example of a company that wants to get employee buy-in and assistance with making the environment an important item on the corporate agenda. When done properly, managing our impact on the environment is good for business. It also wins us accolades from external agencies and compliance bodies, as we show that we are running our company in a way that is sustainable and minimises harm to the communities we work with. And when we win accolades from external agencies and compliance bodies, our clients are impressed and we win more business. Indeed sometimes, it's a minimum standard for doing business with us.

This all makes a lot of sense, so why don't many employees buy into the idea? It could be that they're just not that bothered about it. They are indifferent. Or perhaps the business case isn't clear? Or maybe it is, but there is no emotional connection for employees, as discussed earlier. They need an emotional message to connect with, and to feel they are part of a community, and a cause.

Employees believe they can make a difference

There may be employees who are fully engaged around the topic we want to create culture change around, and these employees really do want to make a difference. They already incorporate environmental activities and practices into their home lives, and are keen to bring it into the workplace. Yet still, they don't engage. Although they want to make a difference, they don't believe they can. Wanting and believing are very closely aligned, and both need to be present for the leadership and the personal responsibility we desire to emerge.

These employees are very aware that they are part of the bigger picture, and are not likely to get involved in that bigger picture if a) their role is not clear, b) management is not setting the right tone for the programme and c) not all company employees are on the same page. To act alone doesn't make any sense. To act together, however, and in a constant and consistent manner, makes a big difference, and employees know this. If what they see and hear doesn't give them the belief that they can make a difference – either personally or collectively – then they won't take personal responsibility. This is a shame, because when we have employees that want to make a difference, a lack of belief can stop them stepping up to lead, and ultimately be the missing link.

Employees know they can make a difference

The third step in showing leadership through personal responsibility is in knowing you can make a difference. So you want to make a difference, you believe you can make a difference, and you also know you can make a difference. If we want leadership and personal responsibility from our employees, we need to give them all three things. As mentioned above, the believing you can make a difference part is quite often the missing link. Very few companies that I have worked with have all three elements lined up, and often the 'knowing you can make a difference' is earmarked for an area of focus, to be addressed through training and communication.

Special training courses can be designed to enhance the skills and behaviours that drive the 'knowing', making sure that all ducks are in a row for leadership to happen further down the organisation. When employees are clear on what behaviours are expected, and they have the required skills to adopt them, then they feel confident, knowing that they can make a difference.

Let's apply a simple three-step process to the environmental example we discussed earlier, explaining what we need to do to create change leaders:

1. **Inspire** our employees to **want to make a difference** – appeal to their values, their experiences, and their identity – make it attractive to be part of an environmental community, to be an 'Environmental Champion'.

2. **Provide** a culture change programme that is integrated and aligned throughout the company, with clear behaviours and expectations, and messages that are constant and consistent – instil the belief in employees that they **can make a difference.**

3. **Equip** your employees with the confidence they need to lead in support of all the above, making sure the behaviours are clear and training is provided for the skills that support these behaviours. Give them knowledge so they **know they can make a difference.**

EMPLOYEE CONFIDENCE RULE 15 – WANT, BELIEVE, KNOW – A RECIPE FOR CHANGE LEADERSHIP

WANT – I want to make a difference

BELIEVE – I believe I can make a difference

KNOW – I know I can make a difference

Transformational Leadership Turns Followers Into Leaders

In the section above, I used the word inspire, because it's a big part of transformational leadership. Transformational leadership is a perfect vehicle for culture change because it cascades leadership down the organisation, in a ripple-type effect, where transformational leaders inspire others to follow them, and those followers to become leaders themselves.

Everyone aligns around a cause

The inspiring has the potential to happen when there is some kind of ethical or moral cause involved, and this is often the case when the cause is people related. Everyone cares about people and their plight, because we are all human beings and have friends, families and loved ones. It is in all our interests to get behind a people cause. That said, not everyone is prepared to stand up for and speak out for a moral or ethical cause because it is easier not to, for all the reasons mentioned earlier. The first step, however, if you want leadership throughout your organisation, is undoubtedly to create that strong moral or ethical cause around the strategic issue in question.

Let's take the Health and Safety example. Every year, according to the ILO[18], there are more than 2.78 million deaths globally from occupational accidents and work-related diseases. This makes Health and Safety a strategic issue for companies, and a matter of responsibility. It requires CEOs, executives and other functions to rally employees around the subject, with a strong ALTE vision, an emotional cause, and a culture change programme as a platform to drive improvement.

Role models become leaders

So transformational leadership turns followers into leaders, and the first step is the ALTE vision, opening the floodgates for leadership from all. The second step is to create role models, because role models become leaders, without seeming to do anything out of the ordinary. Purely through their role modelling behaviour, others will look up to them and follow them, and the transformational leadership ripple effect begins.

When someone adopts highly ethical behaviour, because they do what is widely considered to be the right, albeit difficult, thing to do, then others are inspired and follow them. Often the 'inspire' effect is so great that the followers decide to lead as well, adopting the same role modelling behaviours and inspiring others to follow them. The effect is like a waterfall throughout your organisation and highly profound.

---

18   ILO – International Labour Organisation

So what is this role modelling behaviour? Well a role model we know is someone that we look up to and aspire to be like, because we admire them. In the case of ethical leadership, we look up to and admire someone who we perceive to be doing the right thing, and in the corporate world this is rare, because of the day-to-day work pressures around them. Whilst I am giving the impression role modelling is easy in the workplace, that's not at all the case, but when done effectively, however, it's extremely powerful.

Let's take employee wellbeing as an example. In this case, role modelling might mean speaking all the time to other employees in a way that makes it clear that the wellbeing of employees comes before anything else at work, including cost and schedule. Many managers do this, but then they undo it all immediately by saying or doing something that makes it clear they didn't really believe in what they said anyway, and employees aren't impressed. Some managers undo all their good work in the same sentence, creating a 'reverse role model' effect that leads to a serious loss of respect. With other managers, they might give a great speech on the importance of employee wellbeing at a meeting, and then ask someone to work late, or give them a ridiculous deadline that creates unnecessary stress. Again, the 'reverse role model' effect!

Followers are inspired to become leaders

When we create a strong and cause-related ALTE vision, and encourage our managers and all employees to adopt role modelling behaviours, then leaders and followers are created. This is transformational leadership because it is where culture change begins. What is important here is to be clear on what the role modelling behaviours are, as for employees these are not always obvious, especially when they get caught up in the day-to-day pressures of business. Sometimes you have to spell it out for your managers, letting them know that it is not OK to give a great speech on diversity and inclusion, for example, as the strategic issue of the moment, and then fail to take questions from any minority groups in the room!

With any issue requiring a strong degree of compliance with procedures, this means espousing and living the policies, rules and procedures, every single day – at work, at home, and when travelling to or from work. Firstly, because it's the right thing to do, and secondly, because you never know who is watching. And we are all setting an example, all the time, with everything we say and do – the only choice we have is whether our example is good or bad.

Not all employees will instantly follow this role model effect and become leaders themselves, so we need to use some other elements of transformational leadership. What we need to do is to pay individual attention to employees, understand them, and challenge their thinking. We can do this quite simply by stopping to have a conversation with them, and asking them a great open question in the context of your culture change. With issues such as Health, Safety, Security, Environment, Wellbeing, Ethics, Quality and more, where the vision might be to become the leader in that field in the industry, many companies require their senior managers to go out and visit the worksites, thereby visibly demonstrating their commitment to the issue in question, so that the workforce can see it is important.

This actual visit is impactful in itself; the very sight of a senior manager, high up in the hierarchy, having made the effort to go out on to the worksite is powerful. There is, however, a way to make it even more powerful, and that is through the questions the senior manager asks. He or she could simply just ask a few questions about the work, or they could ask a question like, 'What do you think we would have to do here to create a world-class Health/Safety/Quality/Wellbeing culture?'

Instantly the employee feels valued, important, inspired and challenged – all in one simple and powerful question. This is transformational leadership, and all the manager has to do is ask the question. The employee's brain will do the rest. In summary, transformational leadership for change is a simple recipe: you inspire people, you treat them as individuals, and you challenge their thinking.

It all sounds so simple, giving employees both the reason and the confidence to become leaders, but in reality, there are many barriers to this type of leadership, which require employees to speak out and potentially confront and challenge others to create change.

EMPLOYEE CONFIDENCE RULE 16 – THE 3 'I'S OF TRANSFORMATIONAL LEADERSHIP

INSPIRE – Inspire employees to get involved

INDIVIDUALISE – Give employees individual attention, and allow them to get involved in their own way

INTELLECTUALISE – Make employees' involvement meaningful, by challenging their thinking

CHAPTER 7

There are many barriers to change leadership

There are many barriers to change leadership. Personality preferences and communication styles have a role to play, or perhaps not everyone wants to be a leader, or feels comfortable with difficult conversations, even when they are critical. A lack of communication skills may get in the way, or a perception around how a person's communication might be received. We fear losing credibility, or breaking a relationship – genuine fears in the corporate world. Sometimes it's just simpler and easier not to speak out, because then we minimise the risk of getting involved in an unwanted situation or conflict, or causing offence.

We have spent a lot of time so far talking about the importance of Employee Confidence in leading culture change. We have also discussed the reasons why Employee Engagement isn't working, and how Employee Confidence can enable leadership to cascade down and through the organisation, bringing all kinds of benefits. But companies struggle to realise these benefits, with not all employees confident enough to lead the change we desire by having the necessary critical conversations, so what's getting in the way?

Personality Preference and Communication Style

Sometimes, it's simply down to personality traits and our preferences for thinking, working and communicating. Although it's clear that we can all develop our personality preferences to be more flexible as leaders, capable of operating in many different styles, we also all have preferences that impact what we choose to do, and not to do. There are three personality preference related barriers to employees feeling confident enough to speak out and lead culture change:

Preference for introversion versus extroversion

Jung's theory of psychological types has three pairs of personality preferences, upon which some of the most popular psychometric profiling tools within companies are based. The most well-known of these preference pairs is introversion versus extroversion. Some of us easily label ourselves into one box or another, telling others that they are an introvert or an extrovert. Others are aware that they can do both – known as an ambivert. Those with a more in-depth knowledge of personality preferences realise that while they may have a preference for one or the other, they can easily do the other if they apply themselves. Whatever our preferences, we are all capable of working across the full spectrum of human behaviours. We are ALLPOs!

We are asking our employees to be leaders, but how does that sit with those who naturally prefer more introvert behaviour? How do they feel about this leadership thing? Susan Cain has written a book on quiet leadership, discussing how to lead from a preference of introversion. And all your employees have the potential to lead equally as effectively, regardless of personality preference and preferred working style.

What is important is that your employees know how to adapt their behaviour and style to the situation, and with culture change we need people to speak out directly to others, regardless of their position in the hierarchy. This requires a special type of leadership and requires standing out rather than staying in the background – an approach not always comfortable for those who prefer not to stand out. There is, however, a far more gentle and humble approach, and we will discuss this later on in the book.

In one company I worked with, there was a culture change programme encouraging employees to speak out to prevent bullying and harassment, and although everyone bought into the idea, not everyone followed through on it, and we wondered why. But when we looked at the personality profile of the whole organisation – a highly technical organisation – the reason was obvious. The personality profiles of most employees showed clearly that the organisation preferred introvert behaviours. And when you prefer introversion, you may prefer to sit quietly in the background and think rather than dive in and have a conversation about an issue.

Preference for sensing versus intuition

The second of Jung's preference pairs is sensing versus intuition. What it means is the difference between how you might prefer to size up, assess and judge a situation. When you use a sensing preference, it means you tend to take in only the facts of a situation – what you can see, hear and feel. When you use an intuition preference, however, you assess the situation by extrapolating from the facts before you to what the facts might actually mean.

In the above example of the company wanting ethics leaders who speak out for employee wellbeing, whenever they witness an instance of bullying or harassment, we might see something different happening, depending on which of these two options are applied. Let's imagine someone has witnessed an instance of bullying and harassment and they have a sensing preference. They have gathered all the facts in their mind and approach the person to have the conversation. All well and good. But what if not all the facts are available, which quite often they aren't? This might stop someone from intervening because they want to have all the facts before taking action, and not all facts are available. This might apply particularly to a manager conducting a leadership visit from the office, who cannot possible know all the background and context to the situation they are witnessing, and won't therefore have all the facts.

Let's imagine the same situation from an intuition point of view though. The senior manager arrives on the worksite, without the full picture of how the site operates and is structured i.e. without the facts. However, this manager has an intuition preference, and tends to trust his or her gut feeling on what is going on around them, drawing meaning from incomplete facts. He or she sees a conversation taking place, and doesn't have the facts to prove that it is bullying or harassment but just has a feeling, a 'hunch', that something isn't quite right. They approach anyway to have the conversation and find out more, without fear of losing credibility.

Preference for feeling versus thinking

The third of Jung's preference pairs is thinking versus feeling. This is effectively the difference between using your heart (feeling) or your head (thinking) to make decisions. Do you make your decisions based on logic or emotion? Of course, often we use a combination of both logic and emotion to make decisions. Think about the last car you bought, and I'm sure there was an element of logic to it, around car size, fuel efficiency etc., added to that strong emotional connection you felt when imaging yourself driving that new car! What we are talking about here is preference, and some people have preferences in different contexts – like thinking in a work context and feeling in a home/family context. It really all depends on the individual and the situation.

Imagine though if you have a strong feeling preference. You are being asked to be a leader and to stand up, speak out and have those difficult conversations. What you might consider before having the conversation is less the logic for having the conversation and more the impact on the person on the receiving end. You don't want to make the other person feel bad in any way, and ask yourself how you would feel to be on the receiving end. This preference to put your heart before your head in a difficult conversation – and some might simply call it empathy – could result in two things:

1. Not having the conversation in the first place, for fear of offending.

2. Having the conversation, but not ending up with a good outcome, because the conversation leads you to a new understanding of how the person on the receiving end is feeling, and you retreat without your intended outcome.

In the example above of speaking out to prevent bullying and harassment, it might result in employees not speaking out in all instances of bullying or harassment, with potential consequences for employee stress levels, mental health and wellbeing.

Communication Skills and Perceptions Around Them

Another and possibly more obvious barrier to Employee Confidence is communication skills – the communication skills required to lead change and to stand up and speak out. In some cases, it is a genuine lack of communication skills, either because they aren't natural to the person, or because they have never had any communication skills training. In other cases, the communication skills do exist but the person perceives there to be a problem with them. Let's look at four barriers we might create for ourselves as employees:

Perceiving the person as a stranger

The first perception that might get in the way of communication is that the person you have to speak to is a stranger. Of course, it may be true – the employee may not know the person or have ever spoken to them before. They also might work in a completely different function or environment, or even a different country, and these things might exacerbate the feeling of them being a 'stranger'. And these feelings may be very present, regardless of whether the employee has good communication skills or not.

As an example of this, I have recently been training NLP[19] (Neuro-Linguistic Programming) coaches to be leaders in changing culture in operational environments. To fulfil this role, they need to be able to go up to anyone on site, regardless of level in the hierarchy, and have a conversation. Sometimes they even go out to other

---

19   NLP – a toolkit of communication and coaching techniques that allows you to use your mind better to achieve your goals and help others do the same

operational sites across the globe, to have the same conversations there. The first thing I taught them was about this perception, and that it would be far easier if they removed the word 'stranger' from their vocabulary and replaced it with 'new friend'. Then all they had to do was find a way to establish rapport with the person quickly so that they felt like a new friend.

Perceiving the person as a friend

The second perception that might get in the way of communication is that the person you have to speak to is a friend. Now this might sound a bit strange to you. I mean, how can speaking to a friend be difficult – surely speaking to a friend makes the conversation easier, doesn't it, since you already know them? Yes, in some circumstances, it might appear to be easier because you feel comfortable approaching someone, and possibly already know their communication style and how they might react. When it comes to critical conversations, however, the conversation might be more difficult, and here is the reason why.

When we need to have a critical conversation with a friend or a work colleague or a peer, then the whole friendship thing might get in the way. The strength of the friendship, or the relationship, might supersede the conversation you need to have and stop you having it. This is when fear of breaking the relationship, and the possible repercussions of losing the friendship, might get in the way. There also might be a fear of not being taken seriously, not because the person is a friend necessarily but because hierarchically the person is on the same level as you, as a work colleague or peer, and might not take you seriously.

Let me give you a real-life example of this. When I trained coaches for a manufacturing site as change leaders for occupational health, the next logical step was for the budding change leaders to go out and have critical conversations on site. The issue that came up, however, was that the trainees weren't comfortable going out to speak to their peers to have critical conversations. The perceived barrier here was that on closed sites such as this one, there is a group camaraderie that exists, a community, a social system with its own set of rules, and if the trainees were seen to be breaking those rules by telling the others what to do, then they would be excommunicated from the social system.

This sounds a bit extreme, but to the trainees it was a very real fear. The way to get round this of course is in two ways:

Firstly, to raise awareness among all workers on site on the need for the change leaders and the type of conversations they would be having. This gets buy-in from everyone up front and allows the new critical conversations to become part of, rather than intruding upon, the social system. Secondly, to encourage the trainee change leaders to recognise that what they are doing is the right thing for all workers, from an occupational health perspective, and that the big issue of everyone's long-term health is the most important part of that system. In addition, it is helpful to encourage the trainees to see that their perception of their critical conversations being badly received might not be reality.

I'm a technical, not a people person

The third perception someone might have around their communication skills is that they are not a people person. I have often seen this happen in environments where technical skills are valued more highly than people skills – the latter being viewed as 'soft' or 'fluffy'. Often the employees have spent years fine-tuning and honing their technical skills, with very little focus placed on communication and leadership skills, and have worked largely as part of a quiet technical team where nothing more has been expected of them.

In the example above, when training the NLP coaches for occupational health leadership on operational sites, the very idea of suddenly having to have all these leadership conversations was very alien to them. To help with this, we started by looking at research which suggests that leaders are made and not born, and that all the best communicators were not naturals but people who spent years studying their art.

This got them thinking that they could easily do the same thing. We also focused on communicating in a different way, in more of a coaching style. This meant approaching others in a humble, curious and non-confrontational way, and asking open questions to get the information they needed and empower and inspire the recipient in the process. The technical, and often more introverted, employees I taught felt much more comfortable with this type of approach, and it also shattered another perception – that communication is all about being a good talker. They discovered instead that others place a lot of value on someone listening and asking the right questions – an approach that these employees felt more than equipped for after the training they had been given.

It's a difficult conversation and I'm not equipped

The fourth and final perception barrier around communication skills that might impinge upon confidence to lead change is that the conversation they need to have is a difficult one. Difficult conversations are traditionally seen as coming under the scope of the Human Resources function in the workplace, and the very idea that every employee should be able to have them is anathema to some. When we call any conversation a difficult conversation, and go into it with this idea in our heads, we set it up to be exactly that. We also question whether we are properly equipped for it.

So again, mindset and what we say to ourselves is a good place to start here. We need to find a way to promote, encourage and possibly re-label these conversations in the workplace if we want our employees to step up and have them. It's all part of the honest working environment we talked about earlier, and what we call these conversations. In the context of a strategic issue such as Health, Safety, Wellbeing, Ethics, Quality, the Environment or Security, where it forms the subject of long-term culture change, I have always called them critical conversations, so that employees realise their value and that they have to be had.

The above recommendations seem really simple but how often do they actually take place? I certainly don't remember the last time I had that type of one-to-one conversation with anyone, except when sitting down with my coach. Imagine how powerful it would be to establish a framework within your company for these types of conversations, and how they would slowly start to establish a new working environment.

There are two things to be addressed here:

1. The perception of the conversation and what we call it.

2. The communication skills required to have that conversation.

When we come to the second one, the NLP coaches I train to lead culture change in operational environments learn the art of building rapport and trust with absolutely anyone, quickly, because this is the key to having a critical conversation. Imagine the conversation is an intervention with someone you suspect to be under severe stress. This is a critical conversation and needs to be handled very delicately, with the actual issue not brought up until rapport has been established.

EMPLOYEE CONFIDENCE RULE 17 – THE SWEET SPOT FOR CRITICAL CONVERSATIONS

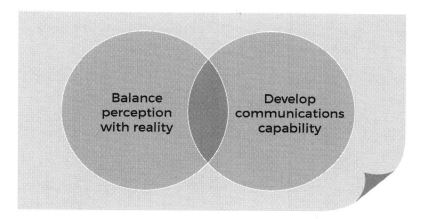

Personal Fears, Perceptions and Insecurities

Regardless of our personality preferences, communication skills and our perceptions of them, there are some other things that affect all of us at some time in our lives, and that is our personal fears and insecurities. Even the most confident employee will experience fears and insecurities around their communication because it's part of being human. And these fears are often heightened when the conversation or communication is deemed to be extremely important, or difficult, or even critical. The three main fears are discussed below:

Fear of losing credibility

The first fear any employee might experience with respect to communication is the fear of losing credibility. When someone is working in a technical industry for example, like technology, engineering, manufacturing or construction, then credibility is often judged on technical criteria, so if an employee doesn't have the full technical information to approach the required leadership conversation, this fear might kick in. We referred to this earlier when we talked about the sensing and intuition preferences, and the sensing approach based on what you can see, hear, feel etc. i.e. what is physically present. This fear may run deeper than preference, however.

I remember one day I was walking an operational site in full safety gear, accompanied by a group of coach trainees, and we were looking for unsafe situations to start a conversation with workers around. I had spent three days teaching the coaches how to do it and now was their opportunity to practise.

Pretty soon I spotted what I perceived to be an unsafe situation, because I saw a large and complex structure that didn't look properly supported, and might pose a safety risk if not positioned more safely. Of course, I didn't have all the technical details and I told my trainees as much. I wasn't trained in that type of work and it was my first time on that worksite. All I knew was that from a big picture point of view it didn't look safe and was worthy of further investigation.

The coaches, however, looked reluctant to get involved without this full technical detail, but I encouraged them to do so. The argument I gave around fear of credibility is that when you approach in a humble and curious way, as per the style more aligned to an introvert preference we discussed earlier, and positioning the worker approached as the expert, a different dynamic ensues. What happens is that the worker responds to the humble tone and the suggestion that he or she is the expert, and is very happy to respond to open questions and give more detail.

The end result is that the credibility thing becomes a non-issue. Since the worker feels important, he or she is very forthcoming – the conversation flows and safety improvements get put in place. A fantastic result from a simple conversation and this is exactly what happened when one of the coaches adopted this approach. Half an hour later we walked past the same piece of equipment and it had been completely reorganised and looked a lot safer!

Fear of breaking the relationship

Another common fear that forms a barrier to Employee Confidence and taking on a leadership role is the fear of breaking the relationship. As human beings, we are hardwired to connect, as mentioned earlier in this book, so the fear of offending, or breaking the relationship, is a very real one. Now if you are a senior manager approaching some workers on site, then maybe you are not too concerned about offending. The purpose of your visit is to promote Quality and you just want to see the job done right first time, and no waste or extra cost. But what if you are a worker approaching one of your peers for a critical conversation on Quality, or even your boss, or the client representative?

This is when the fear of breaking the relationship can halt all critical conversations. Rather than showing leadership skills and speaking up for the right thing, employees do anything to avoid the critical conversation and just do what their boss or the client representative wants. Even with peers, there is no way a worker wants to break the relationship when it's people they work with every day and might even have a close friendship with. We discussed this earlier when we talked about perceptual barriers to having critical conversations.

In the example of the new coaches operating on the operational site above, I taught them how to have a critical conversation without breaking the relationship. Key to a win-win conversation where all parties find an agreeable solution at the end is the coach's ability to build instant rapport with anyone – strangers, work colleagues, bosses, subcontractors and client representatives. And here are some tips for doing it:

1. **Observe** the general demeanour of the workers and adopt a similar style

2. **Approach** with welcoming, relaxed body language, and smile

3. **Open** the conversation by introducing yourself and letting them know you are interested to find out a bit more about the work they are doing

4. **Position** them as the expert and yourself as the curious party, asking lots of open questions beginning with What and How

5. **Notice** any common ground that comes up and highlight it to the other party

6. **Discover** more about them by asking what they like most about the job

The above six tips are only small things and may sound obvious, but they are extremely effective if your culture change leaders want to be successful with their critical conversations i.e. get the required outcome without breaking the relationship.

EMPLOYEE CONFIDENCE RULE 18 – A CHECKLIST FOR CONDUCTING CRITICAL CHANGE CONVERSATIONS

Observe the general demeanour of the workers and adopt a similar style

Approach with welcoming, relaxed body language, and smile

Open the conversation by introducing yourself and letting them know you are interested to find out a bit more about the work they are doing

Position them as the expert and yourself as the curious party, asking lots of open questions beginning with What and How

Notice any common ground that comes up and highlight it to the other party

Discover more about them by asking what they like most about the job

Fear of speaking in front of others

Another fear that gets in the way of Employee Confidence for change leadership is a speaking-related fear, and it sometimes depends who is in the audience. It's fear of public speaking but can strike even when speaking on a one-to-one basis with others around you, potentially judging you. It can strike in meetings, when you know and have been working with the attendees for months, but the thought of speaking out in front of them is asphyxiating.

The fear of public speaking, or 'glossophobia', is well documented. According to a research survey in the US, fear of public speaking is the biggest fear of all, coming even before the fear of death.

In the UK, research suggests it's the second biggest fear people have after spiders. What is less documented is that fear of speaking out in small groups, such as a meeting, when you are not even at the front of the room giving a presentation but simply giving your comments from the back of the room. In a way, it's fear of speaking out from the audience.

I remember once being in an extremely long meeting and noticing that several participants were starting to flag. They were standing, rather than sitting, stretching their backs, and the ones that were still sitting looked tired and were struggling to concentrate. We had been working for a long time without a break and I felt it was time to take one. The meeting organisers, however, seemed focused only on the agenda and the work still to be completed. I took a deep breath and decided to speak out, but the organisers didn't appear to hear what I had said and just kept on going. I felt really embarrassed, wondering what everyone was thinking of me, and attempted to fade into the background. As I said, speaking out isn't easy and comes with a certain element of personal risk.

It's Easier Not To Speak Out

In the above example, it would have been easier not to speak out at all. And there are many reasons why employees don't actually speak out, even when they want to, and four of the most common ones in my experience are detailed below:

Speaking out takes time

So why is it easier not to speak out? Well firstly, it takes time. And what I mean here is preparation time. Some of us speak off the cuff, without giving it a second thought. Others of us do give it a second thought, and a third, and a fourth. In fact, when there is a critical conversation to be had, we like to take our time to plan out what we are going to say, and that time is not always available to us.

In the example of the long, tiring meeting I talked about earlier, I was busy planning the conversation in my head for a good five to ten minutes, and during that time I was clearly not really paying attention to everything else going on in the meeting. The urge to do the right thing was taking me over and my head buzzing on how best to approach the matter.

When the conversation is critical, however, like suddenly seeing a need to intervene on a worksite for a security reason, there isn't always time. For example, if you suddenly saw a stranger without a security badge walking unauthorised around company premises, and you are worried they might injure themselves or other workers, you might need to just stride over there as quickly and calmly as possible and escort that person off site. In a different situation, for example where the identity of the person was uncertain or they appeared to be emotionally volatile, then the conversation might need a little more thought, and that would require more time.

I remember when I was working with someone and I started to worry about them being under too much pressure, and that they might be bottling it all up. Where this person had previously been very happy-go-lucky, he became withdrawn and miserable overnight, and was rude to the people around him. I knew that I had to speak to him to find out what was going on, but given his behaviour and the sensitive nature of the topic, I needed time to think through the best approach. And time is a scarce resource in today's workplaces.

Speaking out is risky

In all the examples I used earlier, the conversation was a difficult or critical one, at least in the eyes of the person thinking about it, and this means that for them there is risk involved. When I spoke out at the meeting to give my colleagues a break, and when I spoke to my colleague under stress, there was personal risk involved in both cases – risk of being perceived in a certain way, as meddling or pedantic maybe, and risk of someone getting angry with me, or the relationship not going well in the future. The second reason for not speaking out is that it incurs an element of risk. One way of managing this risk is to ask yourself, or encourage your change leaders to ask themselves, two key questions:

1. How important is this conversation?

2. How much risk is involved?

I have compiled a little 2 x 2 matrix in diagram 4 below to help us with handling critical conversations like intervening and stopping the job for a critical issue (Safety, Health, Ethics, Wellbeing, Security etc.) – something you can run through your head every time you feel stuck and in a quandary over whether to have the conversation or not.

If your conversation is of low importance and low risk, you probably wouldn't bother having it because it's not important. The same goes for low importance and high risk. If, however, the conversation is high importance and low risk, there is nothing to stop you having the conversation immediately. And when the conversation is classified high importance but also high risk, you might need to plan it carefully, recognising its importance but at the same time mitigating that risk.

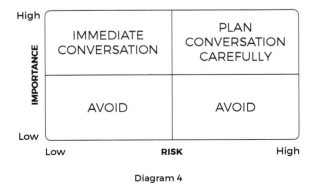

Diagram 4

EMPLOYEE CONFIDENCE RULE 19 – STRATEGIES FOR CRITICAL CONVERSATIONS

Low importance + low risk = Avoid

Low importance + high risk = Avoid

Low risk + high importance = Immediate conversation

High risk + high importance = Plan conversation carefully

Speaking out might incur further action

There is a third reason why someone might not want to speak out, even if it is the right thing to do, and that's because the conversation might incur further action. We have considered carefully the need to have the conversation and how we are going to do it, and this has already taken us some time. We feel confident the conversation is the right thing to do and that we know how to handle it. But what if it starts off a process that is going to require even more involvement from ourselves and more action? We can't start something so important and then not see it through – our conscience wouldn't allow it!

In the example of the friend I approached with concern about their behaviour and the potential mental ill health behind it, the conversation went well, with the person welcoming the intervention and speaking openly, but then of course I couldn't stop there. I had opened the conversation and then felt compelled to see it to its conclusion, checking on that colleague on a regular basis. Leaving it at the first conversation would have been easier, but with the right communication toolkit, further conversations do not necessarily have to be a burden and give your employees a chance to lead change.

Speaking out might conflict with social norms

The fourth reason why it might be easier for someone not to speak out might be cultural rules. An employee might feel personally that intervening for worker health, safety or security, or escalating an ethics issue for example, is the right thing to do, but from a cultural point of view, to directly confront someone about the problem is not at all acceptable, especially if it means crossing the hierarchy i.e. speaking to someone higher up in the organisation than you. In some parts of the world these types of cultural barriers do exist, but rather than get in the way, they can be harnessed.

In fact, these cultural barriers do not dictate that you can't speak out, only that speaking out needs to be done in a culturally accepted way. Often we forget this when designing our Employee Engagement programmes and asking our employees to be leaders. We dictate a certain way of doing things when a more flexible approach is required, allowing our employees to show leadership in a way that is comfortable to them.

When working with operational sites with a multicultural workforce, I heard this type of story many times. We were encouraging every single worker to feel empowered to intervene any time they felt a risk to employees existed, but we were mandating a particular approach. We were asking the workers to directly approach the person and have the conversation, but many of the workers felt uncomfortable with this due to cultural constraints. When we realised that some cultures were collectivist[20] and with a high power-distance[21] ratio, as per Hofstede's classifications, we knew that employees would not feel comfortable speaking out directly, so we changed our approach.

We changed our communications campaigns for interventions, suggesting various ways to intervene, including creating and emphasising a 'trusted advisor' role for someone to go to, where culturally appropriate. We also emphasised the benefits of the approach to the group, since within collectivist cultures, group interests predominate over individual ones.

Confidence is required to overcome fears and take a personal risk, but it's worth it. When employees feel comfortable with the potential consequences of taking the risk, or that they can mitigate it, they start to speak out, and collectively they build a culture of confident change leadership.

---

20   Collectivist – operating as a group and emphasising the interests of that group

21   Power-distance – the extent to which less powerful members of organisations accept that power is not distributed evenly throughout the organisation

CHAPTER 8

Employee Confidence creates culture change

Employees have their own control panel for confidence, made up of beliefs, feelings and behaviours, and when all three are aligned, they positively impact others and start to create a ripple effect. Other employees are inspired, more critical conversations ensue, and confidence becomes the key ingredient for team and company effectiveness. A confident environment is the final element in effective culture change, acting as a mirror to the employee's own confidence control panel – reflecting the same confidence back to employees and enabling them to flourish. Line managers are key players because of their ability to influence up and down the hierarchy.

Confidence works at many different levels within an organisation, because confidence exists, or not, within individual employees, and interacts with the confidence levels of other employees. When employees are confident, this has a positive impact on the confidence of the employees around them, and vice versa. An employee's confidence is also impacted not just by that of other employees but also by the environment in which they find themselves, composed of the beliefs, feelings and behaviours of the people that form that environment.

We All Have a Control Panel For Confidence

When it comes to change leadership in particular, which comes from the heart, then we all have our own control panel for confidence. This control panel consists of three elements – beliefs, feelings and behaviours – and these are likely to be misaligned in some employees. Some effort is needed to get them in alignment, because they have an impact on others, and sometimes just an awareness of the existence of the control panel is enough to make a difference. Your employees' control panel for confidence is composed then of not three but four key elements:

1. What they BELIEVE

2. What they FEEL

3. How they BEHAVE

4. The IMPACT that all the above has on other employees

We feel according to what we believe, we behave according to what we feel, and our behaviours impact others. Together this creates an aligned confidence control panel for leading culture change and the impetus to do it. Let's look at each element in turn:

EMPLOYEE CONFIDENCE RULE 20 – THE CONFIDENCE CONTROL PANEL

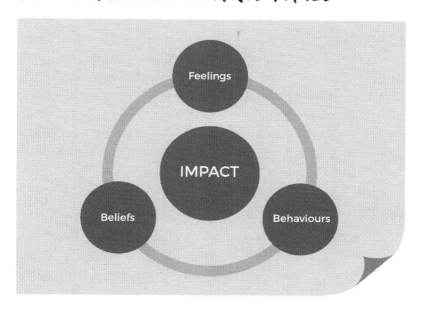

We need to have the right beliefs

Leadership starts with what we believe. Beliefs are our rules governing what we will or won't do and are allied strongly to our personal values – so important to us that they become our personal deal breakers. Let's imagine someone has a strong value around fairness. If we perceive a company not to offer us fairness or to operate in a fair manner, we might choose to leave it or feel really uncomfortable staying. In this example, fairness has become our deal breaker and has several rules (beliefs) associated with it, such as everyone having the same amount of office space or flying the same class of air travel, for example. These beliefs drive confident actions and decisions, giving us our sense of what is right or wrong.

Let me give you an example. All accidents are preventable. This statement is a belief and whether it's true or not isn't relevant. What is relevant is what the belief leads to. When we believe that all accidents are preventable, we are likely to be more proactive, more attentive, and more of a leader when it comes to putting in place behaviours and systems to prevent every possible injury or illness. Whether we can control everything that might happen to us or not is irrelevant; the law of probabilities says we have much more chance when we have a prevention mindset that leads us to prepare for all potential accidents. So what our employees believe is going to impact the extent to which they feel confident, show leadership and lead change.

We feel according to what we believe

What you believe is going to affect how you feel and that will drive your behaviour, so feelings are part of the employee's control panel for confidence. Employees are expected to be logical and rational at work, and to suppress their emotions, but whether we acknowledge them or not, our feelings are always present, are often based on beliefs, and will drive behaviour. In the context of changing culture, if employees believe in the cause, and feel they can make a difference, then they will act to ensure it. I remember coaching someone to have a critical conversation to address regular offenders on a worksite flouting the security rules, with a negative impact on the prevailing culture. When the worker in question was hesitant to get involved, he said it didn't feel right to be telling his work colleagues what to do. I asked him what this feeling was based on, and he said that it was based on the fact he didn't believe he would have any impact. When I delved a bit deeper, it turned out that this person had tried to have a conversation about it previously, and the workers laughed and just kept on doing the same insecure behaviours, so he no longer believed he had enough credibility to make a difference. Without the belief, the feeling was of uncertainty, and the behaviour one of inaction.

So I asked him if there was ever a time when someone did listen to him and find him credible, and he was able to give me a whole host of examples, like the time when he once came up with an idea for a new badge system to make the workplace more secure, and he got a special commendation from management. It's worth remembering here that often we base our beliefs on one simple event in the past that didn't work out well, for whatever reason. And then we make an unconscious decision to adopt that belief for the rest of our lives, based on one single event, and that decision can limit our potential in the future.

We behave according to how we feel

So now we get to behaviours, the visible part of an employee's control panel for confidence. Behaviours can take on many forms. They may be simply conforming behaviours, where rules are followed and standards adhered to, and these behaviours are critical to leadership for culture change. In large companies in all types of industries, processes and procedures on critical issues like Health, Safety, Security, Quality, Ethics etc. are extensive and mitigate risk, so following them is essential. And although these may on the face of it seem like simple conforming behaviours – nothing out of the ordinary – when they are done in support of an emotional cause, like any critical issue affecting people then conforming is role modelling, and role modelling is leadership.

Change leadership starts with these simple conforming behaviours, and encouraging others to do the same. These behaviours follow the same sequence, based on the employee's belief that he or she can make a difference, and a belief in the purpose and robustness of the procedures. So belief is the starting point and gives the employee a feeling of confidence and comfort – enough to take action and adopt new behaviours.

Sometimes, however, complying and following the rules is not quite as easy as it sounds. When working in closed operational environments, where the same employees are together for long periods of time, then the environment is more than a workplace – it's a social system. Relationships, networks and pecking orders are established, and peer pressure exerts itself heavily on employee beliefs, feelings and behaviours.

I remember going out to a construction site to deliver some culture change training, and during the training itself, when we discussed as a group what we might do to improve employee Health and Safety, the subject of consistent rule breaking, or taking shortcuts, came up. Everyone agreed that taking shortcuts was unacceptable, and that doing so was putting workers in danger, but no one wanted to take a stand. This was down to peer pressure and the relationships and friendships being stronger than what they knew to be right. It was also down to camaraderie, bravado and complacency. Without addressing these basic conforming behaviours, how could we hope to get on to the more inspirational behaviours, around conversational coaching? What was the point of going any further? And I told them so.

Whichever way we look at it, everyday behaviours form part of the employee's control panel for confidence, and we need to be clear on a) what we want to see and b) what beliefs and feelings we need to address first.

Our behaviours impact others

The fourth and final element of the employee's control panel for confidence is impact – the impact that employees' beliefs, feelings and behaviours have on others, which is not often recognised. We are not always aware of our employees' beliefs and feelings because they are not always visible, although sometimes betrayed through our words, our body language and our behaviour.

In fact, it's this latter part – our behaviour – that is the key to understanding impact on others, because it's the most visible part of the first three elements of the employee's control panel for confidence. How we behave leaves an impression on others and impacts our own confidence system i.e. what we believe, how we feel and how we in turn behave. Now you can see that if we want a certain culture, we are going to have to reach a critical mass of employees adopting the behaviours that define that culture.

Malcolm Gladwell in his book *The Tipping Point* called this phenomenon a tipping point – the point at which enough people are doing the same thing to influence the whole system. When companies want to build culture, however, it's not just about the number of employees all adopting the same behaviours, because the organisation has a hierarchy, with those higher up having more power than those lower down. So when more people higher up are adopting the behaviours, this is likely to have a bigger influence on the system, and the culture change, than if more people lower down adopt the change. This also works within sub-systems, such as closed worksites and independent regions and business units.

An example of this is where a senior manager of a large company is photographed visiting one of his or her sites and obviously flouting one of the rules around a critical issue – no safety helmet or no security badge for example – during a leadership visit. This failure by one senior manager to adopt required behaviours could have a big impact on overall behaviours. Only one person, and only one behaviour, but massive impact on the beliefs, feelings and behaviours of others, due to their position and influence in the organisation.

The Confidence Control Panel Starts the Ripple Effect

We talk about confidence having many different interrelated elements in a company, and each employee having their own confidence control panel, composed of beliefs, feelings and behaviours, and which, when aligned, impacts others and drives the required change. When all employees have their confidence control panels aligned, and aligned to the needs of the company, Employee Confidence builds and starts to create culture change. It is a single employee, then, with their confidence control panel fully aligned, that starts the ripple of change, for three key reasons:

Confidence is required for critical conversations

It is a single employee with an aligned confidence control panel that starts the change, because critical conversations cannot be had without confidence on the part of the person approaching the conversation. They need to have confidence that:

a.   they are doing the right thing

b.   they can communicate effectively for a win-win outcome

c.   they won't offend the other party in the process

The employee's confidence control panel acts as a driving force, a propeller, where everyone is prepared to start the confidence ripple effect throughout the company by being the one to step up, and have that critical conversation when required. Let's imagine one such critical conversation. An employee perceives that a team is being put under undue stress, due to increasing workload and long working hours. He or she knows that to speak out is the right thing to do for employee wellbeing. But the employee won't speak out because they don't believe they have the power to change the system and feel they won't be listened to. And so the system doesn't change.

I have seen this happen, and as a single individual we often feel we don't have enough power to change a system, but it works like a waterfall, with a single drop of water eventually leading to a full-on gushing waterfall and a brand new system. Of course, everything needs to be lined up – the timing and the approach need to be right – but one person, with their confidence control panel aligned and activated, can make a difference. Recognising this is the starting point and empowering others to get involved comes next.

Critical conversations impact team effectiveness

The employee's confidence control panel is the driving force in the culture change system because employees rarely work in isolation – they work in teams. It only takes one individual to show change leadership for another team member to follow. And another, and another, until the whole team is behaving like confident change leaders. It also acts in reverse. When an employee's confidence control panel is neither aligned nor activated, they shy away from taking action, hoping that someone else has seen the problem and will do something about it.

One day, for example, I was working in an office and I remember a guy making an offensive comment to one of the women working there. He just threw it into the conversation as if it was perfectly acceptable. I was astounded because it was only the week before that everyone had been asked to sit a mandatory e-learning module on preventing bullying and harassment in the workplace, as part of a new global campaign. The girl just seemed to shrug it off, and no one around her said anything either. I was a few desks away and was sure that they all must have heard what I heard. But they didn't appear to, at least not for a good five minutes. And the offensive comments just kept coming. I stepped out of the office to go and say something, but before I got there someone else finally realised it was time to say something and walked up to the offending employee. All it took was that one action, from an employee with a clearly aligned confidence control panel, and beliefs, feelings and behaviours around respect for others, and a precedent was set for team culture, standards and acceptable attitudes and behaviours.

Critical conversations enable company effectiveness

Companies are composed of teams and functions, and quite often the latter operate as independent and quite isolated units, as discussed previously with the examples of operational workplaces. Sometimes it's because they are simply more remote from the rest of the organisation and sometimes it's because they prefer to keep themselves that way. Even with teams working in geographical proximity, the emotional distance between them can be enormous. This is the silo effect, where teams operate under their own rules and agenda, without too much thought to the big picture, and often competing or conflicting with the aims of the wider organisation.

When a team of employees does not have their confidence control panels in alignment, with themselves, each other and the company, and its members are not stepping up to the plate to lead the change, then they often turn inward. They focus on their own micro-environment and their own issues, where a more confident team might collaborate with other teams rather than compete with them, to the detriment of the overall aims of the company.

With the team I trained on the construction site that couldn't initially get over the hurdle of addressing the basic conforming behaviours, and eliminating the corner cutting, they were also very protective of their own environment. A lack of confidence alignment as a team caused them to look inwards rather than outwards, whereas contact and collaboration with a similar site in the same company, with similar problems, might have enabled joint problem solving to the benefit of the company.

Team confidence alignment, or a lack of it, impacts cross-team collaboration and company effectiveness, and is a driver, or not, of culture change and a one company approach.

A Confident Environment Enables Employee Confidence to Flourish

We have looked at an employee's own control panel for confidence, and the importance of achieving alignment, and if we can do this for every single employee, won't that lead to a confident organisation ready to change culture? Well, yes, it may well do. The more confident employees we have, the more they start to work together, as we discussed earlier, and build confident teams and eventually a confident organisation with a fresh new culture. There is, however, an additional role to play to create the confident organisation – a role that every single person can play – and this will further strengthen individual confidence. We need to collectively create the environment that enables Employee Confidence to flourish, and there are three main reasons why:

A lack of confidence is fear based

A supportive environment is the final key element in the Employee Confidence system because lack of confidence is fear based. Let's consider that the organisation acts as a mirror to individual behaviour. In simple terms, when Employee Confidence is encouraged, through a supporting environment, then Employee Confidence is further boosted. And that environment comes partly from the culture change that starts to build through Employee Confidence, and partly through the establishment of additional 'supportive' behaviours, which need to be considered.

Lack of confidence is a problem in reaching the critical mass required for culture change, and it is based on fear, as we discussed earlier. Our role as a company is to create the environment that makes that fear irrelevant, so that the confidence, and the required behaviours, can flourish.

There was one company I knew that was big on employee health, and an employee survey indicated that stress was a problem, probably down to all the change happening at the time. Employees felt uneasy and uncomfortable as restructuring was taking place and some job roles were being made redundant. The company's management in some regions saw the stress issue and launched local campaigns to do something about it. The campaigns encouraged workers to speak out to line management if they were worried about their own stress levels, or that of colleagues, but very few had the confidence to do so.

Fears are often based on an expected external reaction

A supportive environment acts as a mirror for the entire culture change system because fears are often rooted in an expected external reaction, and when the latter isn't positive, confidence isn't reflected back to the employee. So why wouldn't people speak out for their own stress levels or those of their co-workers? The message from top management was clear – managing and reducing employee stress levels was a priority – so what was stopping them? Whether concerned about yourself or someone else, the issue of stress is a very sensitive one; mental ill health not only has social stigma but can also negatively impact an employee's career.

There is a genuine fear around speaking out for any kind of strategic issue, and people issues in particular, as discussed earlier, with fear of breaking the relationship being one of the bigger ones. In general terms, the fear is around the expected external reaction, and in an example like this it is highly complex. Although senior management are clearly stating that the issue is important, and they want people to speak out, there may still be a lack of trust around managers taking the issue seriously and keeping it confidential.

Speaking out may also start a chain of external reactions which lead the employee into further difficult conversations, and may impact relationships or even their future career prospects.

A confident environment provides the required safety net

A confident environment acts as the mirror for Employee Confidence because it reflects confidence back to the employee, letting them know it is in alignment with their confidence control panel. It also provides the required safety net, as mentioned earlier in the book. Speaking out on an issue such as stress – or any important people issue for that matter – requires a safety net, and the company needs to not only put that safety net in place but also communicate clearly that it exists. But what does this safety net consist of?

When we expect employees to behave like leaders on certain issues, and to speak out, we must accept that we are asking them to take personal risk, and not everyone is comfortable with that. As we know with risk taking, sometimes we win and sometimes we lose. And when it comes to critical conversations, we want to make sure it is a win-win, so that the risk is eliminated, or at least mitigated against. Diagram 5 below shows that whether this win-win happens is a function of two factors: shared importance of the issue and empathy with the other person.

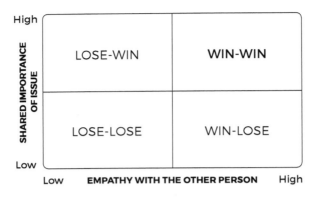

Diagram 5

If we decide to speak out for stress, we need to feel confident that the issue is of shared importance – to me, to the other party and to the company. So shared importance of the issue is high. We also need to feel confident that we have empathy with the other person, if there is one involved, and that we have taken time to understand their position and thought through how they might feel. In any other scenario, where one of the elements is low, then one party will lose.

Companies need to consider this element of personal risk when introducing their leadership campaigns and aiming for culture change. A confident organisation acts as a mirror to Employee Confidence, so as a company we need to act in alignment. And when we do, this provides the required safety net for the personal risk. This safety net is the win-win that comes from your change leaders having a high level of empathy with others, and dealing with issues that have a strong shared importance. Whatever method you choose, you need as a company to cultivate both.

EMPLOYEE CONFIDENCE RULE 21 – THE SAFETY NET OF CULTURE CHANGE LEADERSHIP

Low empathy + low shared importance =
Lose-Lose

Low empathy + high shared importance =
Lose-Win

High empathy + low shared importance =
Win-Lose

High empathy + high shared importance =
Win-Win

Line Managers and Supervisors are Key Players in Confidence

There are a number of different ways a company can provide a safety net for personal risk taking, and line managers and supervisors can be key players. This is down to their position in the organisation. They are not right at the top of the hierarchy and neither are they down at the bottom. No, they sit right in the middle, with exclusive access to both senior management and the workers. Because of this, they have to communicate regularly – upwards and downwards – and have the ability to influence positively, or negatively, at all levels. Line managers and supervisors, with their ability to influence up and down the hierarchy, are key players in the Employee Confidence system and for three main reasons:

They create Employee Confidence opportunities

Line managers and supervisors create confidence opportunities for employees. Remember earlier we talked about 'stretch' activities, essential for personal growth and confidence? Well, line managers and supervisors can create these stretch activities and confidence opportunities. They can do this for example by encouraging their workers to take on more responsibility and to learn new skillsets. To do this, they need to be able to delegate and to not feel threatened by the growth of their employees, and for this they need confidence.

Let's see how that might work. Very often at work we have set meetings we are required to attend, and often they follow the hierarchy, depending on the culture of the organisation. There is, however, nothing to stop line managers and supervisors from delegating their attendance at a meeting from time to time to one of their employees, to create that confidence opportunity for them. Or they could attend alongside one of their employees and let that employee do all the talking, with the safety net of having you alongside them. I remember one manager I had allowing me to do this and it was very empowering. The thought that your manager trusts you to do all the talking is very inspiring and confidence building. It's also an opportunity for you to be a bit more visible in the company, which builds your credibility and your confidence

They impact employee belief structures

We need to provide opportunities for Employee Confidence, and line managers and supervisors can do this through how much of the work they keep for themselves, how much they delegate, and how much of the talking they do at meetings. We mentioned earlier that behaviours all start with belief. We need managers and supervisors to believe that all their people have potential and to act in support of this by creating opportunities for them.

Line managers and supervisors can also have a strong influence on the beliefs of their employees. They can make or break belief structures among employees, and recognising this means that as a CEO, senior business leader or HR director, you can do something about this. And here is a practical example.

When I was delivering leadership training to site workers at an energy company, we started a discussion on what coaching was, using several different definitions of coaching, written on pieces of paper on the floor, to help us. As we worked our way around the group, stories started to emerge of how individuals had either been coached themselves or had successfully coached others, and what had really made the difference. One guy told the story about how he had started out as an apprentice in the oil and gas industry, and had been working offshore for the first time. He had been trained how to do his job but hadn't really put his skills into practice on site before and was very nervous.

He remembers not wanting to show anyone his nerves or insecurities, but fortunately for him, his new boss picked up on them without the new guy having to make any kind of statement. "Don't worry," the boss said to the new guy, "I know you can do this, mate." With this language, the line manager created the belief and the confidence within the employee that he could proceed. As senior business leaders, then, it is important that we inform our managers about the big difference they can make to their people, and often just through a slight change in language.

They also provide a safety net

Line managers and supervisors are key to the culture change system because often what we need as employees is simply a safety net for their personal risk, as discussed earlier. For most of us, when we are learning new skills and taking on new activities – whether these be technical skills like welding, or new leadership and communication skills – we can get most of the way by ourselves. Yes, for most of us, we can get 90% of the way there, until we suddenly start thinking about the risk involved, and then we start looking around for a safety net. It's the safety net that provides the support for that last and critical 10% of the journey required to complete the new action, or the critical conversation required for culture change.

A few years ago, I found myself on a charity dance challenge, and unexpectedly part of a circus performance in Brazil, with the proceeds going to help the street kids. We trained together as a group – a mixture of professional circus performers and amateurs like me – to put together a credible circus performance in just two weeks. I had several different roles in the performance, including a five-minute show on the trapeze. Despite my dance background and reasonable amount of strength and flexibility, performing on a trapeze was not something I could just do, like that. I received a lot of training, and sometimes I wondered if I would ever get there when my body was exhausted and every muscle aching. What got me through it, though, was the safety net, and not just the actual, physical net below me. I'm talking about the safety net provided by the instructors and coaches who provided a system and a belief structure that got me that last and critical 10% of the way.

The same goes for the confident environment in our companies. One way to give employees a safety net to behave in a confident and leader-like way is a buddy system. When I introduced an integrated coaching programme across an entire manufacturing site in South America a few years ago, I noticed that employees I trained were looking for confidence to go out and try out their new skills, on critical conversations for safety culture change. They had got 90% of the way there themselves, by attending the training and paying full attention, but that final 10% was a bit elusive. So we set up a buddy system, and got them trialling the new skills in pairs, with each pair giving each other feedback. This allowed them to try out their new skills and develop their confidence in a safe environment before going it alone and becoming culture change leaders.

CHAPTER 9

Creating the confident and influential employee

Confident and influential employees have four key types of confidence – Internal, Deep, External and Strategic. Equipping your employees with all four gives you human capital that is confident, fulfilling their potential, influential and high performing. For internal confidence, teach them the power of the four selfs – self-understanding, self-acceptance, self-challenge and self-cheer. For deep confidence, show them the power of purpose, mindset and positive internal conversations. Boost their external confidence with training on how to use the right words, voice and body language. Unleash their strategic confidence by preparing them to tackle any critical conversation with skill and dexterity.

In the last chapter we talked about the employee's confidence control panel, and to align its individual elements, with themselves, others and the company, and supported by a confident environment. And all to the benefit of a confident culture. Now we are going to take things to a whole new level. We are going to look at individual Employee Confidence in a more in-depth way, breaking it down into a four-part model for long-term confidence, influence, performance and results.

Internal Confidence is the Foundation

Let's start with creating internal confidence. How do we turn our employees into true leaders without position power in your workplace, able to tackle anything they put their mind to, including all those critical conversations, and always knowing the right thing to do and how to operate at peak performance? Internal confidence is composed of four key elements:

It starts with self-understanding

The first self of internal confidence is self-understanding. Whether you are an employee reading this, or a senior business leader, confidence starts with self. When I say starts with self, what I mean is that we need to understand ourselves, and especially the full power of our brains. In most companies today, except possibly the creative industries, employees are left-brain dominant, approaching work with logic, sequence and analysis, and little emotion. There is of course nothing wrong with this because we all need to use our left brain to be calm and reasoned and analyse the facts of a matter before making any kind of sensible proposal.

But what about the right brain? Are your employees using this part of their brain as well? In today's workplaces many of us (depends on the industry and profession of course) are not using our right brain enough. When we are very left-brain dominant, we tend to overthink things, take our work home with us, and struggle to switch off. I'm not suggesting we quit using our left brain, because it's essential to our work and has served us very well. But what if we were to use our right brain in equal measure and unleash the full power of our minds?

I remember training a group of software engineers in presentation skills, but this wasn't any old presentation skills course, it was a little bit different. It was teaching them how to deliver authentic presentations using both left and right brain techniques, getting more out themselves and having more of an impact on the audience. I knew that they weren't going to engage unless I spoke to them in a left-brain way, so I taught them a left-brain process for learning the right-brain techniques. And when they practised the right-brain techniques, they noticed it switched off their left brain for a while, giving it a chance to recover, giving them new ideas, or solutions to problems they had been trying to solve for days.

Self-acceptance comes next

Once employees start using their left and right brains in balance, they become more accepting of themselves. As they start to use their right brains, they become more open to imperfections and let the unimportant stuff go. To use their right brains effectively, employees have to first switch off their judgmental left brains.

Self-acceptance is also about accepting all of you – warts and all. Self-acceptance is not just important for an employee's own confidence, but also for their ability to influence others. This is because when someone becomes more accepting of themselves, they become more accepting of others, making way for everyone to operate at peak performance.

One exercise I get employees to do to enhance self-acceptance is to write down a list of all the traits that annoy them in others at work, circle the word that causes the biggest emotional reaction, and ask themselves why. You can also do this exercise yourself, or with managers, and I would recommend you do. Often this new understanding completely removes the negative emotion and energy from the word, allowing the person to focus instead on more positive things, like performance and results.

Self-challenge helps employees grow

The third self of internal confidence is self-challenge, something we mentioned earlier in the context of stretch activities, to keep employees learning, growing and growing in confidence. When I am working with people, I take any opportunity I can to stretch myself, and those I am working with, albeit with a safety net in place, as I realise that challenging yourself can be scary. In fact, many people just won't do it unless pushed. They'll take the easy way out and simply decline or delay.

In my work training coaches for culture change, I teach a one-day course that simply teaches employees to have the confidence to connect with others, so that the difficult conversations seem a little less difficult. When I teach it, everyone buys into the thoughts and ideas straight away, as they seem so simple and so obvious. What they don't realise, though, is that by the end of the day they are actually going to be using the skills they only just learned a few hours earlier, and communicating and connecting with others, with confidence.

I ask them to work in groups for the last hour and a half, planning a presentation around how the new skills could be applied on their worksite, and then they have to actually stand up and give the presentation. I don't mention this when I assign the task, but they pretty soon realise that if they are presenting ideas to use their new 'connecting' skills, then they have to challenge themselves and stand up and talk about it in a way that connects with others. Self-challenge is essential for internal confidence and peak performance.

Self-cheer builds momentum

The fourth and final self in internal confidence is self-cheer. Your employees need to remember to cheer themselves on and celebrate their achievements – something we don't do enough in the workplace. Sometimes it's because we don't have enough time and other times we just set ourselves impossibly high standards. We tend to focus instead on all the things that haven't worked out well or the things we did wrong.

Let's say you give a presentation; you may have done 99 things right, and been very well received, but instead of focusing on this you focus instead on the one thing you did wrong, or thought you did wrong. Maybe it was the section you missed out, the question you didn't have the answer to, or the moment you tripped slightly on your words. Or maybe it was the moment you wobbled slightly when reaching for your prop. Whatever the little thing was, it seems to have taken on gargantuan proportions in your brain whereas those wonderful 99 things you did have just disappeared into the ether.

Good leaders, however, need perspective on their own achievements, and to help others to do the same. Sometimes, however, our brains have already been trained to look for errors and defects, for example in some technical and engineering roles. So what's the solution?

If your employees' brains are wired to look for the one negative needle in the haystack of positives, then we don't want to change this because it might be a skill much required in the workplace. What we need to do, however, is to bring balance and ensure employees can take another perspective in different contexts, and particularly in the context of change leadership.

What we do then is to get employees to train their brains to examine the haystack itself from time to time. When they finish an important activity, and are doing all the post-event analysis in their brains, get them to write a list of all the things that went well and all the things that didn't go well, starting with the positives. There will always be as many positives as negatives, sometimes more, and when employees find the positives, they need to cheer themselves on and acknowledge their success. Self-cheer is essential to internal confidence and change leadership because it maintains momentum and enables employees to ride out the confidence dips.

Deep Confidence Creates Energy

The second type of confidence is deep confidence, and deep confidence comes once internal confidence has been achieved. Its drivers are authenticity and purpose, which is why people with a purpose seem so much more authentic and confident than those that don't. Think about how you feel those times when you really believed in something you were doing, and how that affected your confidence and your ability to stay motivated even when the going got tough. There are three elements to deep confidence:

Purpose comes first

Deep confidence in your employees can come from having a cause, working alongside all fellow employees, as one strong unit or community, to achieve something great together. If it's something they really buy into, like keeping everyone safe every day in a hazardous working environment, then it's really going to drive their confidence in the workplace.

Deep confidence also comes from living in line with your values. When you live and work in line with your values, you get a sense of confidence and comfort that everything is as it should be. When your employees know what their values are, this gives them purpose, direction and confidence. And when managers also know the values of their team members, they can give them work that aligns with them, allowing them to achieve their potential.

Personal responsibility is essential

Having a mindset of personal responsibility is important for deep confidence. Confident employees show leadership, and leadership means action and having those critical conversations even when they are uncomfortable. Leaders don't delegate critical conversations to others. They take personal responsibility for fixing problems that shouldn't be there, from a moral and ethical point of view.

Taking personal responsibility is far easier for employees when they have internal confidence. When they understand themselves better, they are more likely to take personal responsibility for anything that doesn't align with their own personal rules for fulfilment.

I remember someone I worked with who never had an issue with having a critical conversation when the health or safety of anyone was at risk. He used to stride right up there to speak to the person in charge, and always seemed to do it in a tactful and diplomatic way so that the potential issue was instantly resolved. He was the Jiminy Cricket of the workforce, acting as their conscience when they were under pressure and reminding them to do the right things to keep themselves safe.

This was personal responsibility, and the more he enacted it and got a positive response, the more confident he felt and the more leadership he displayed. He also looked confident in the eyes of his fellow workers, and they were inspired to follow suit.

Channel self-talk for a positive outcome

The third and final part to deep confidence is being mindful of how you talk to yourself. Yes, of course you talk to yourself. We all do. But the question here is, how do you talk to yourself? Are you nice to yourself or do you beat yourself up all the time, with that little parrot that sits on your shoulder and says 'That wasn't great!' or 'You won't be able to do that!' or 'That's never going to happen!'

If you want deep confidence for your employees, you need to encourage them to get that nasty parrot off their shoulder and replace it with a lovely singing bluebird that sings out nice encouraging words like 'You've got this! You can do this! Just do it!' They need to visualise the singing bluebird there instead of the nasty parrot, or whatever makes sense to them, and allow their self-talk to become more positive and motivational. These mental performance skills are not new, it's just that we rarely apply them in business.

How employees talk to themselves internally is a key barrier to, and driver of, confidence. With the right self-talk, they will overcome their own limiting beliefs and put the leadership skills you are asking for into action. They probably won't admit this to you, but it's the nasty parrot on their shoulder that won't let them step up to the plate, and the singing bluebird that will. That's why I make sure that when training employees as coaches, and equipping them with the skills to have critical conversations, the first critical conversation they need to have is with themselves.

Before they even consider how to approach the conversation, and what they are going to say, I ask them to reflect on what they would need to say to themselves to increase their confidence going into the conversation and make it more likely to lead to a positive outcome. If there are any negative phrases in there, I get them to rephrase their self-talk and reframe it in the positive. I also get them to visualise themselves knocking the nasty parrot off their shoulders with a big red boxing glove and allowing the singing bluebird to fly in and land on their shoulder instead.

None of this may sound logical but that's because it isn't. Logic is the domain of the left brain and what I am talking about is right-brain techniques like visualisation – a vital ingredient in the mental performance skills today's change leaders require. Confidence is more than just logic for our employees, it's about getting the maximum from both left and right brain skills, and the latter are particularly useful for overcoming fears and achieving a positive outcome, on every occasion.

External Confidence Influences Others

The third type of confidence is external confidence. When companies want to give their employees more confidence, they tend typically to focus on this area i.e. presentation and public speaking skills and how employees present themselves to others, both inside and outside of the organisation. Rarely do companies focus on the other areas of confidence discussed in this chapter. When external confidence skills are preceded by high levels of internal and deep confidence, however, the overall level of employee confidence is higher, and the potential to achieve and influence greater. External confidence has three key elements:

Words and language

Speaking confidently is often what will get your employees noticed within the company and outside of it with your partners and contractors, and you want to make sure that they are saying the right things. This part is very much about the words and can largely be catered for through consistent and constant communication at all levels on company messaging. When it comes to functional and departmental presentations, senior managers and line managers will have a strong input.

On top of this company-specific content, there are some global rules for communication that can help your employees communicate in a more confident and leader-like way, and influence others:

1. Give your REASONS at the beginning of the presentation – why what you are presenting is important and what difference will it make if they get involved.

2. Give POSITIVE (not negative) messages – discuss what you want people to do (not what not to do) and talk about scenarios that will make them feel good; when employees feel good, they are inspired and want to be involved.

3. Use language of options, choice and POSSIBILITY – everyone likes solutions but no one likes being told what to do.

Voice volume, pitch and intonation

How your employees deliver their message is as important as its content, and maybe more so. Can you imagine someone saying all the right things to you but in a total uninspiring way – drab, monotone voice that you can hardly hear, and intonation that constantly goes up at the end of the sentence and makes the speaker sound uncertain? The way we use our voice is a key determinant of confidence and how confident we make others feel.

This also works inwards as well as outwards. Try speaking to yourself in a tiny, drab, monotone voice which wavers, crackles and often goes up at the end of a sentence. How confident do you feel now? Now try the same thing, speaking to yourself in a louder, more certain voice, possibly deeper in pitch, varying in a melodic way but going down at the end of every sentence. I expect you are feeling a lot more confident than with the first voice. A confident voice not only makes the person speaking more confident but is also contagious, inspiring confidence and leadership in others. Voice influences!

I remember training someone to deliver culture programme training to the workforce and his voice was the only thing we focused on. I felt that focusing on the way he used his voice in delivering the session would make the biggest difference to his performance as a trainer and his ability to influence others, and it was. We showed him what to do, gave him strategies to sustain the change, and everything else followed suit.

The right body language enhances authenticity

Another key element of the impression you give to others when you communicate and how much confidence you create is your body language. There are whole books dedicated to the subject of body language but here we are going to focus on its influence on authenticity, which is really important for employee confidence. Authenticity comes from being true to your values, and when employees communicate in terms of their values, this will show up naturally in their body language and will cause them to inspire and influence others unconsciously.

There are two ways employees can consciously use their body language to appear more confident and influence others. The first way is congruence – aligning body language with their words. This will happen naturally when they believe in what they are talking about, but employees can also consciously use gestures that emphasise their words, thus increasing their authenticity in the eyes of the audience. If talking about integration, for example, they may bring their hands together, or if talking about leaving old habits and behaviours behind, they might point behind them or to one side.

The second way is by appearing balanced and centred, literally. When you are speaking to an audience, this means standing still and centred, with equal weight on both feet, and looking straight ahead. I remember once watching a senior manager delivering a talk on the importance of Ethics, and he paced back and forth the whole time. Not only was it distracting but it made him look nervous, and I personally started to question the strength of his conviction on the topic. When you are physically balanced and centred, you unconsciously appear stronger, and your credibility and influence is enhanced.

Strategic Confidence Takes Confidence to a Whole New Level

So we examined three types of confidence – internal, deep and external – and all three together are more than enough to create confidence in your employees. There is one final confidence type, however, and this one is critical in a corporate environment, and not usually on our people development radar. It's called strategic confidence and equips employees to maintain their confidence in all situations, particularly in critical and transformational conversations, and always gets a win for themselves and the company. Strategic confidence is the ultimate influence for positive behavioural change and is broken down into four parts, known as the four Ps:

Teach employees to prepare for conversations

The first P in strategic confidence is Preparation. We may already have confident employees, but how do we know they are prepared for the ultimate test of confidence: succeeding at critical conversations for culture change? The other party in the conversation is never completely predictable, but we have more control if we manage out any unpredictability in advance. And we do this by planning out the conversation in our heads and going through a cycle of stages which can be run once or several times until we have all the information we need to be well prepared. Being prepared is important for confidence and ensures we arrive at the conversation with the right mindset and the right message.

Let's imagine running through the cycle in the context of planning an intervention with a client on some work that is going on that isn't following occupational health procedures and therefore is putting workers at risk. Clearly this is going to be a critical and a difficult conversation, given that it is with the client. Your employee knows their own point of view, and how you feel about it, but do they really know the client's point of view? How much understanding do they have of the other party's position? And is their own extreme focus likely to cloud their judgment?

The cycle has four stages, and you can set them out on the floor in front of the employee quickly, with labels on four pieces of paper, and walk them through the four stages. Alternatively, you can run the exercise verbally, on the phone even, asking open questions to glean the right information for each stage.

So what are the four stages in the cycle? Well, the first one is Focus, where your employee goes for what they want. The second one is Empathy, where they consider the position of the other party. The third one is Impartiality, where they imagine they are independent and can see both sides of the conversation. The fourth one is Learning, when they stop to consider what insights they have from the previous three stages. When your employee forces themselves to really think through the stages in this cycle, the right approach to the conversation will become clear. It's a great technique to help our employees prepare for critical conversations. Once they know it, employees can run through it on their own, or ask a colleague to coach them through it. The technique is extremely powerful and it gives employees confidence to lead the culture change the organisation needs.

EMPLOYEE CONFIDENCE RULE 22 – A PREPARATION CYCLE FOR CRITICAL CONVERSATIONS

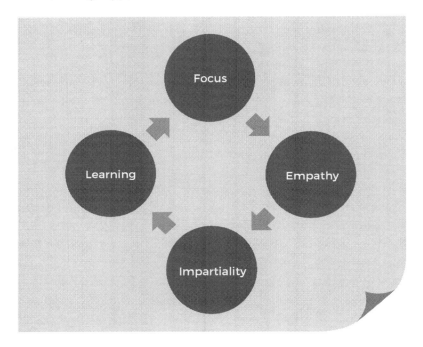

Show them how to present the right proposal

The second P in strategic confidence is the Proposal an employee makes to the other party during their critical conversation for culture change. They need to make sure they have a win-win proposal for the other person or people in the conversation. When a win-win proposal exists, employees will feel more confident because they will know they have a proposition that will benefit both them and the other party. The other party will also have confidence in your employee because they have bothered to consider their needs and come up with something that addresses them. Now let's look at what constitutes a win-win proposal.

Stephen Covey in his book *The 7 Habits of Highly Effective People* dedicates a whole chapter to win-win thinking and defines it as a function of courage and consideration – courage to state what you want and consideration of the other party's point of view. In the context of confidence, win-win thinking is simply coming up with a proposition that inspires confidence on both sides. Earlier on I asked you to run your critical conversation through a four-stage preparation cycle to make sure that you had all the necessary insights before approaching it. At stage two, Empathy, you would have understood where the other party was coming from. Then at stage three, Impartiality, you may well have seen something that makes sense to both parties. This is the win-win you are looking for.

I remember advising a company on how to create more personal leadership among their employees in the context of Environmental Protection, and they couldn't really get anyone excited about the whole Environment thing – it really needed selling. So I decided to run through the four-stage critical conversation preparation cycle with the team, and what came up was that the employees didn't want to take on another company initiative, they were on initiative overload. Then when we got to stage three, Impartiality, we saw that what made sense was to just have one Health, Safety and Environment leadership programme, integrating Environment into the existing Health and Safety programme. This was the win-win and the environmental team proposed it to management.

Equip them to position themselves for rapport

The third P in strategic confidence is Position and this means how your employees position themselves during a conversation. Let's imagine they've already planned their conversation well and considered it from the four stages of the preparation cycle, as mentioned earlier. They've adjusted their message based on the insights gleaned. They feel confident that their message is going to get through and are ready to have that critical conversation. What else could they possibly need? Well even if they have planned their conversation comprehensively, and know that they are a confident communicator, they still have a job to do to establish that trust required for the person they are talking to to be responsive and listen to what they are saying, without taking offence. What they need to do is to be able to position themselves to connect instantly with anyone.

There are many techniques you can use to establish a connection with someone, just one person, but what if you need to establish a connection with a whole group of people, as fast as possible? Here you really have two choices: either you find a common connection with every single person in the room, quickly, or you find a connection with the opinion leader in the group and let them do the rest.

Both techniques are effective, and one fast way to establish rapport with a group is to find out how they generally greet each other (very useful when working globally across different cultures), and to learn how to do this in advance. Create an opportunity for this greeting very early on and get everyone greeting each other simultaneously, including you. This will create a moment of rapport, when trust is established and the foundation is laid for great communication. The other option, creating rapport with the opinion leader, might just be a case of doing some research to find out what is important to that person and how they like to work.

Teach poise and flexibility of communication

The fourth P in strategic confidence is Poise. When your employees have prepared their conversation in advance, positioned themselves well for connection and rapport, and the communication has begun, what happens then? Now, since they are so well prepared and able to communicate with confidence, the conversation will go exactly as they expect, won't it? In fact, they can probably almost predict the way it is going to play out and all they need to do is stick to the script, don't they? Well, the better prepared they are, the more likely it is to go as planned, but really all the preparation does is give them confidence to get the win-win outcome. To manage the critical conversation effectively, poise is required.

Poise means remaining calm and in control, and balanced and centred, regardless of what the other person in the conversation does. The other person may say or do something you are not expecting, but you expect the unexpected and take all this on board calmly. And the thing you don't expect may also be something happening in the background, and regardless, you need to remain focused on your conversation and move to a new location if necessary and possible.

Poise also means being flexible and prepared to deviate from the plan if required. So how will you know if you need to deviate from your plan? To know this, you need information. You need to read the signs. All the time you are talking to the other person, or people, he or she, or they, will be giving off minute body language and facial gesture signals that let you know if the message is getting through. And if you detect it isn't, or that further convincing or clarification is required, simply press pause on your talking for a moment and ask a question.

I remember a time when I was giving a presentation to a senior management team and it was going really well. I knew this because I constantly scanned the audience for their body language and read signs of engagement among all of them. That was until suddenly one of them asked me a question. And what he said was this, "Are you taking feedback now or at the end?" I could see from his sudden change in body language that waiting until the end was not an option for him, so I replied, "Now, of course, go ahead." Had I not read that signal quickly, the presentation would have gone downhill, because his doubts, and me not taking feedback until the end, would have impacted its success. It was poise that gave me strategic confidence and made me much more influential, whatever resistance I encountered.

EMPLOYEE CONFIDENCE RULE 23 – CREATING THE CONFIDENT AND INFLUENTIAL EMPLOYEE

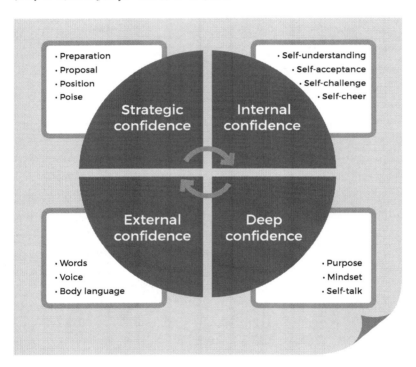

CHAPTER 10

Making Employee Confidence stick

Making Employee Confidence stick in your organisation is essential if you want to realise the full benefits of human capital operating at peak potential. It's a four-step process, starting with an assessment of the fears stopping your employees having the confidence to lead change, and then addressing them through the training of change leaders and establishment of worker-led Employee Confidence networks, so that Employee Confidence also builds from the ground up. The real building, however, occurs in step three, where confident behaviours are clearly defined and managers trained to support them. Employee Confidence finally starts to stick at stage four, when behaviours are made specific to job role, we measure our overall progress and are able to adapt to exceptional situations.

Companies don't just need confident employees, they need this newfound Employee Confidence to become embedded so that it becomes an integral part of the company culture. Only then will Employee Confidence lead to the long-term human capital value and performance it is designed to deliver. To embed Employee Confidence, however, requires the level of Employee Confidence reaching a 'tipping point', as discussed earlier. What follows is a four-step approach to reaching this tipping point as quickly as possible and making Employee Confidence stick.

STEP 1 - ASSESS

The first thing to be done is some assessment – to find out what the main fears are in the organisation so that they can be addressed and largely eliminated. In Chapter 7 we discussed some of the fears that might get in the way, and when we get out there and speak to people we can get a better idea of exactly which ones might be driving certain undesired behaviours and preventing the leadership ones we want. Employees won't always tell you their fears directly, but you can learn a lot from their language and behaviours.

Fear of being judged or criticised

The first one is fear of being judged or criticised for saying or doing the right thing. This may simply be personality-led, and a fear that someone has, irrespective of where they are in the world, but it can be exacerbated by the organisation and/or job role they are in, and can also be alleviated by changes to the culture of the organisation.

When someone fears being judged or criticised, they tend to 'walk on eggshells'. This means that they tread very carefully with everything they do, and in treading carefully to avoid doing something that could lead to judgment or criticism or 'breaking the eggs', the irony is that they often make more mistakes than they would have done without taking this extra care. Other visible behaviours around this fear might be refusing to speak out, support or escalate issues, and instead choosing the middle ground, or 'sitting on the fence', in an attempt to keep everyone happy.

The judgment or criticism could come from just one person within the organisation, and sometimes it can be removed easily by removing this one person. I once spent some time at a worksite, for example, trying to understand their culture, when I noticed that this fear was very real and came from the autocratic style of the site supervisor, requiring everything to be done in a certain way, at a certain time, with no room for error. When rules and procedures are enforced without trust and supporting language, then this fear emerges and can be very counterproductive. In this case, strict attempts to enforce rules and procedures led to less of the required behaviours, not more.

Fear of losing one's job

The second fear getting in the way of Employee Confidence becoming embedded is the fear of losing one's job. I don't believe this fear is as widespread as it might have been a few decades ago, because of the societal changes referred to at the beginning of the book. People in general have far more options for bringing in an income and aren't confined to just one permanent job. As we said above, more and more people are going freelance, particularly women, and adopting a portfolio lifestyle or career. That said, the fear of losing one's job is still out there and particularly in certain situations.

One such example is an industry-specific crisis or more generalised country downturn, where companies are driven to restructure, reorganise, downsize and/or merge with other companies to survive. Survival becomes a modus operandi, for employees as well as their companies, and it is driven by the very real fear of losing one's job. Companies are obliged to be transparent with their workers and go through a consultation process on redundancies, so often employees are aware well in advance of the likelihood of job losses. This fact only serves to exacerbate the fear and uncertainty for those going through the process and awaiting a decision.

The fear of losing your job will lead to different behaviours for different people. Some will seek out alternative employment, and usually the most talented employees, as we said earlier. Some will retreat inwards and work even harder, losing confidence and internalising the pressure until one day something snaps. Others will start vigorously protecting their work or over-promoting themselves to justify their job roles. All of these behaviours, if left unchecked, can lead to mental ill health, whereas if addressed can be converted into Employee Confidence.

Fear of breaking the relationship

The third most common fear, and again one we mentioned in Chapter 7, is the fear of breaking the relationship, and is in some cases connected to the fear of losing your job. For example, if you are living with the fear of redundancy, then your behavioural strategy may be to over-network, preserving all the relationships you possibly can, to make sure that when redundancies happen, your job is not one of them. This behaviour pattern may also be stress-inducing as the employee seeks to maintain their job workload and their network. In big project industries, where the stakes are high because expensive equipment is being operated and the cost of delays and downtime is extortionate, the pressure to comply is also high. This may lead to a culture of complicit rule breaking and shortcuts, and people not wanting to speak out, even for something as important as the health, safety and security of the workers. This could be a fear of losing their job at the extreme, but at the very least it is a fear of breaking the relationship first and foremost. No worker on a billion-dollar project wants to break the relationship with a client of the company.

The three fears described above can be standalone, but also sometimes be interrelated. Fear of breaking the relationship could be driven by the fear of losing your job, as described above. It could also be driven by the other fear – fear of being judged or criticised. If, for example, employees are working with someone that operates in a very autocratic style and doesn't like to be challenged or questioned, doing so could realistically lead to a break in the relationship, hence the fear.

Of all the behaviours described above, the most significant for Employee Confidence will be employees not speaking out and not having the necessary critical conversations, because if they don't, they won't be leading the change your company needs to succeed.

STEP 2 – ADDRESS

You don't need to be an organisational psychologist to identify the fears listed above, but simply be able to notice the behaviours described and ask yourself why someone might behave that way. It is important to address the fears at the root of any behaviours that are counterproductive to desired company culture and performance. To start to embed Employee Confidence, what is needed is a critical mass of employees adopting and exhibiting the required leadership behaviours, as quickly as possible. To achieve this, we need to create ownership of the approach among employees and a group of employees acting as enablers. Managers can also accelerate the approach. These three elements are discussed in the sections below.

Train key personnel as confidence coaches

First of all, we train key personnel as confidence coaches so that these key personnel can act as early adopters and enablers of the Employee Confidence approach. They champion the approach and encourage others to adopt, by helping them to overcome their barriers to adoption and convincing them of the benefits of the change.

We select key members of staff across the company who are already influential and early adopters of any change, and give them a special identity as 'change agents', 'confidence buddies' or 'Employee Confidence (EC) Coaches'. Think carefully about the language of this identity and what will resonate with the people involved. Make it both motivational and clear. These early adopters are tasked with adopting the new leadership behaviours and coaching others to adopt them as part of their daily job roles.

Once we define and communicate our required behaviours for our desired culture change, a significant proportion of employees will change anyway, but some won't. There may be pockets of the organisation where the existing culture is firmly embedded, and change is going to require an extra effort. With operational sites I have worked with across several different industries, we empowered key site personnel to become change agents and gave them the skills to drive the change. These skills included the ability to recognise internal barriers in individual employees and help them push through them to adopt the required, rather than the fear-based, behaviours.

Establish worker-led Employee Confidence networks

So far, we've created our change agents, confidence buddies or EC coaches, with the aim of ensuring widespread adoption of the desired leadership behaviours. Whilst culture change may be led principally from the top of the organisation, we can accelerate adoption and the resultant culture change by empowering employees to drive the change at grass roots level as well, thereby ensuring a two-pronged approach. Employee Confidence is more likely to become embedded in the organisation if it is advocated for and driven both from the top and the bottom of the organisation.

To create ownership of the change from the bottom of the organisation requires a degree of trust and a sense of autonomy. Employees need to trust that the whole organisation, and especially management, is behind the change, and that the change is around for the long term. No one will take the time and effort to change the way they work if they think that this is purely a short-term initiative and that something else will be required of them in six months' time. Employees will take ownership of the change if they are involved in the change from the outset and are offered a certain degree of autonomy.

Create a proposal for the culture change and the leadership behaviours required and present it to the workforce in your different entities. You will have already chosen and trained your confidence buddies and they can help to get buy-in at this stage. You might even ask them to present the proposal. Present your proposal on culture change for the workplace as a proposition in a format that is only 70% complete and requires the workforce to take it and provide the final solution – the final 30%. It will then feel like their project, but you will still have had a say in the main direction and requirements.

EMPLOYEE CONFIDENCE RULE 24 – GETTING BUY-IN FOR CHANGE

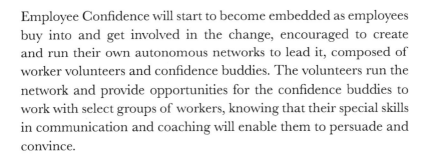

FOLLOW THE 70-30 RULE

70% of proposal put forward by you

30% of proposal completed by employees

Employee Confidence will start to become embedded as employees buy into and get involved in the change, encouraged to create and run their own autonomous networks to lead it, composed of worker volunteers and confidence buddies. The volunteers run the network and provide opportunities for the confidence buddies to work with select groups of workers, knowing that their special skills in communication and coaching will enable them to persuade and convince.

One practical example of this type of worker-led network would be a system for peer-to-peer safety observations on a worksite, with a worker committee set up to conduct the observations and pioneer the change, and an additional managerial committee set up to assist with the implementation of proposed improvements. Key change agents led by the worker committee act as 'safety buddies', observing behaviours, giving feedback, removing barriers, and getting agreement for the required change.

Train managers in critical conversations

With the two actions described above – the training of specialist confidence buddies and the establishment of autonomous worker-led networks – Employee Confidence will start to spread throughout the organisation, as the new leadership behaviours are adopted quicker and by more people. What we need to do now is to make sure that this momentum is supported, and even accelerated, by supportive managers. The confidence buddies, and other workers, will have the confidence to have the critical conversations required for change, and managers will provide the environment to keep it moving.

What we need to do then is to train our managers to give them an awareness of the approach to be taken by the confidence buddies, and the worker-led networks, the kind of critical conversations they will be having, and with whom, so that the managers know a) what to expect and b) how to support them. Managers need to know their role so that they don't become the blockers when workers propose their ideas upwards, as a result of the work of the confidence buddies and the worker-led networks.

In my experience, the biggest problem these worker-led networks come up against is being able to 'sell their ideas upwards'. This depends partially on Employee Confidence to attempt to influence, and partly on the communication skills to do this effectively, but manager response is also important. Manager response can be either supportive or not so, and if not so, this is not always intentional. What's significant, however, is that when employees have the confidence to adopt a new approach for the first time, and the conversation or action is not supported by their manager, then they are unlikely to try it again.

How we might train managers to be supportive to the change is by involving them in a workshop based on the critical conversations that need to take place in the context of the culture change. For example, for Health and Safety, it might be intervention or stopping the job for safety. For Employee Wellbeing, it might be conversations around stress management and resilience. For Ethics, it might be a conversation around a potential bullying, harassment or bribery issue. The four-stage critical conversation preparation cycle described earlier can be used effectively to get a comprehensive understanding of how a critical conversation might go – from Focus to Empathy to Impartiality to Learning – before the right approach is agreed.

STEP 3 – BUILD

When you establish a worker-led network of confidence buddies (or change agents) and get management thinking about their role in the critical conversations that require confidence and leadership, then we are already starting to build a culture of Employee Confidence and the change it will drive in your organisation. To formalise it, however, we need to ensure all the elements are in place to build that workplace environment we talked about earlier in the book – the honest working environment where employees feel valued, listened to, encouraged and supported. What specifically do we need to do to build this kind of environment, to build a culture conducive to Employee Confidence?

Define behaviours for valuing others

We need first to be clear on how we want all employees to act to show that they value others, but what specifically do we want them to do? If we follow the transformational leadership model, ideal for culture change, then employees become followers and then leaders themselves when they feel inspired, are given individual attention, and their thinking is challenged. To achieve this, we need managers to adopt behaviours such as those listed below with all their direct reports, without exception:

1. Schedule face-to-face time (or video conference time) with your direct reports at least once a month.

2. Inspire them by communicating or recalling the vision for the company and where they fit into that.

3. Interest them by asking open questions around their strengths, skills and ambitions.

4. Stimulate their thinking by asking them questions that solicit their ideas e.g. 'How would you put that into action? What if we wanted to do X, how would we achieve it?'

In summary, schedule time with them, inspire them, interest them and stimulate their thinking.

The above recommendations seem simple, but how often do we see them in the workplace? Imagine how powerful it would be to establish a framework within your company for these types of transformational conversations, [22] and how they would slowly start to establish a new working environment.

EMPLOYEE CONFIDENCE RULE 25 – THE SIIS RECIPE FOR TRANSFORMATIONAL CONVERSATIONS

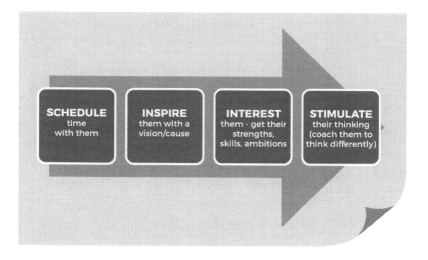

SCHEDULE	INSPIRE	INTEREST	STIMULATE
time with them	them with a vision/cause	them - get their strengths, skills, ambitions	their thinking (coach them to think differently)

---

22   Transformational Conversations – conversations that change behaviours

We also need to give our confidence coaches a framework around which to conduct their own transformational conversations so that the behaviours for valuing others and changing behaviours trickle down the organisation. In my own work training confidence coaches in a culture change context, I have created a framework within which they are free to use their open questions as long as it more or less follows the sequence. It is based on the widely adopted coaching GROW (Goal, Reality, Options, Way forward) model developed by Sir John Whitmore in his book *Coaching for Performance* and goes something like this:

What do you want to achieve at work?

Where are you right now with it?

What's getting in the way of your progress?

How could you move forward?

What's the first step?

EMPLOYEE CONFIDENCE RULE 26 – THE CONFIDENCE BUDDY'S TRANSFORMATIONAL TOOLKIT

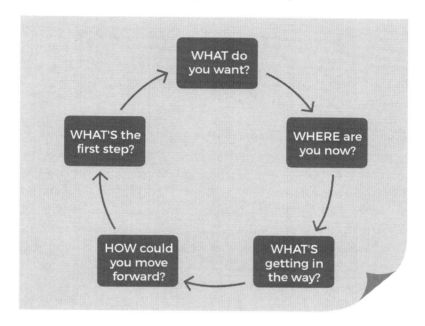

With this simple What, Where, How and What cycle, the confidence buddies are able to take colleagues naturally and easily through a conversation that will inspire them, challenge them, help them progress and adopt the required positive behaviours, and make them feel valued. These five questions are the confidence buddy's transformational toolkit.

Train managers in effective listening

There is of course one skill that is critical to these kinds of coaching conversations, the kind that inspire confidence in employees, and that is the ability to listen. If a manager is not able to sit back and really listen to the answers that come back from their direct reports, and incorporate what they hear into the overall structure of the conversation, and the next question, then the whole conversation will be ineffective.

Being able to listen effectively is the missing link in the cycle. With it, the conversation will flow and the employee will feel more and more valued at every step, and more progress towards a win-win solution will be made. Without it, the conversation will falter and bits of information will be lost or misinterpreted, causing the result to be less than it could be.

There are many courses on effective listening, and they can easily be made mandatory to all managers, with monitoring to ensure the skills are put into practice. Despite this, employees and managers still struggle to listen because so many things get in the way. It could simply be all the many distractions in the workplace, but often it is the employee's internal voice running, either consciously or unconsciously, and seeking any number of things more important to them than the incoming information. From attention to progress to judgment and dominance, any number of agendas stop us truly listening like we need to, to be able to communicate and influence in a confident manner.

Effective listening needs awareness and constant practice. With one company I worked with, we combined the right-brain activities with active listening in one training course and discovered that this was highly effective. When employees turned off their logical, rational and judgmental left brain and their associated internal voice in order to use the right-hand side of their brain, then their mind really cleared. Suddenly they were able to really listen to what people were saying to them.

To really value employees, then, we need to:

a. Give them the time

b. Ask them the right questions

c. Listen to the answers

d. Flex our output to match the incoming information

EMPLOYEE CONFIDENCE RULE 27 – FOUR RULES FOR CONFIDENT LISTENING

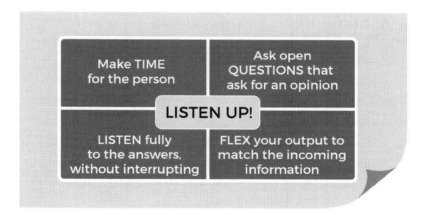

Build 'encouragement' elements into reward systems

In the earlier sections of this book we talked about encouraging our employees to set personal goals and even to establish a personal potential plan, and that this personal potential plan should include stretch activities. Whatever you decide to designate as encouragement activities, these need to be designed, documented, formalised, incorporated into the various systems, and then communicated. If you make these a suggestion, or a nice to have, then they probably won't happen. If you make them just optional tick boxes on your managers' forms for their appraisals, then they will run out of time and probably not end up including them. Personal potential plans also need to be measured and reported on.

If we are serious about this Employee Confidence business, and changing our culture so that we elevate our levels of personal leadership, then we need to see the following indicators on our boardroom scorecard:

Personal Potential plans - % complete against target

If we want our employees to reach their potential, resulting in a massive leap in Employee Confidence, productivity, employee retention and business results, then we need to measure it at board level. The above indicator measures only the quality rather than the quantity of the plans, but it is a great start!

Train and reward managers to support the new employee behaviours

As a final recommendation for building this new culture, this honest working environment where employees feel confident because they are valued, listened to and encouraged, we also need to ensure that they are supported. As mentioned earlier, this is important because employee behaviours do not occur in isolation, they impact on and incur a reaction in others, and usually as part of a critical conversation. Sometimes this reaction comes from peers, but more often it comes from managers, so managers need to be clear on how to respond to the new confident leadership behaviours.

Earlier on in the book we discussed the kind of supportive behaviours we needed for this new confident culture. We also talked about how managers could provide support for critical and even transformational conversations. Now let's look at how managers generally can support the change starting to happen among their employees and support their employees to drive that change.

As soon as managers start to notice the new behaviours emerging, it is really important that they respond in the right way and thus provide positive reinforcement. Specifically, we need managers to:

a. Welcome the new leadership behaviours

b. Take time to understand the work their employees are doing to drive the change

c. Look for opportunities to promote the employee upwards and make their work recognised and visible

This is the Managerial Change Support Triangle, as seen in the diagram below:

EMPLOYEE CONFIDENCE RULE 28 – THE MANAGERIAL CHANGE SUPPORT TRIANGLE

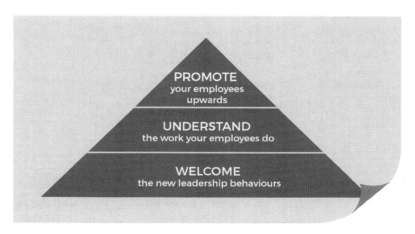

So how do we build these supportive behaviours and embed them into the overall culture change that is starting to take place? Well some of it is simply a matter of training, and I know from experience that when you train managers in coaching skills, it not only makes them more interested in people but also improves their communication and listening skills and encourages them to have conversations that are more supportive to their employees. So this is one thing you can do – give your managers coaching skills.

If you want to reinforce the behaviours in this triangle, you might also think about what you recognise and reward in your managers. Could we consider rewarding them not just for their own performance but also the performance of their team members as individuals? Could we also consider an employee rewards programme for the new leadership behaviours we want them to exhibit, or even a team competition on the critical conversations declared as required for the culture change, where the number and the quality of such conversations are recorded and recognised? In the example of stopping the work in the case of an Environmental risk, we could record not only the fact that the conversation had happened but also its quality i.e. measures such as whether it resulted in:

a. an Environment-critical piece of previously undeclared information being uncovered, and/or

b. a change in the work process that minimised risk of damage to the Environment

STEP 4 – BLEND

The final step in making Employee Confidence stick is blending together all the individual elements that we have discussed so far. Imagine you get up one morning and go to your fridge. It's full of fresh fruit and vegetables and you know you have all the ingredients you need for a healthy start to the day. It's only when you put them all in a blender, however, and blend them all together into a tasty smoothie, that you have a final product and the full potential of all the ingredients can be realised. The nutritional value from all the individual ingredients blended together is greater than that of all the ingredients separately, purely because you are more likely to ingest it.

The same goes for Employee Confidence. This book has given us all the elements we need to consider and put in place, but the real power of these elements only comes when we make an extra effort to blend them together, making Employee Confidence stick and ensuring all parts of the system are working together. What we need is confident employees, confident teams and a confident organisation, creating a culture of leadership and influence that drives peak performance, and to get it there are four more things to do:

Provide a clear matrix of behaviours

When it comes to aligning the system for confidence, the first thing we need to do is to provide a clear matrix of behaviours. If we have a culture change programme ongoing, or are about to start a culture change programme, we need to be clear on exactly what behaviours we are looking for. We mentioned previously the idea of establishing some clear leadership behaviours for all, like see it, say it, sorted (the railway example).

This tryptic of behaviours is very memorable from a marketing campaign point of view and everyone understands broadly what they are required to do. There may, however, still be a level of detail required to be explicit. A few bullet points under these behaviours will make it crystal clear what you might see, what you need to say and to whom, and how exactly the problem gets sorted. Without these details, the request for the leadership behaviours may still be ambiguous and not get adopted by all, at all levels.

When you are looking for confidence to change the culture in your organisation, you may also be looking for some more extensive behaviours, and this will need to be lined up across the organisation. For example, let's say you were looking for culture change for the strategic issue of Gender Intelligence, and one-key behaviour was to be a role model and inspire others.

When you look across the organisation, however, role modelling would be enacted differently depending on job role. Senior managers, for example, would role model by conducting leadership visits and sponsoring Gender Intelligence sessions. Supervisors would role model by always talking about Gender Intelligence at meetings. Workers would role model by always complying with the Gender Diversity policy and suggesting work improvements that would support it.

The full power of culture change is unleashed, and Employee Confidence embedded, when a clear matrix of behaviours is provided, allied to the required culture change and showing what is expected of everyone, at different levels of the organisation. When everyone can see what is expected of them, and where their behaviours fit in the big picture, AND what everyone else is expected to do, then motivation and confidence increases. This also makes the culture change far more visible and easier to measure.

EMPLOYEE CONFIDENCE RULE 29 – A BEHAVIOUR FOR EVERY JOB ROLE

	Behaviour 1	Behaviour 2	Behaviour 3
Job role 1	X	X	X
Job role 2	X	X	X
Job role 3	X	X	X

Provide training and communication at all levels

Secondly, we need to provide training and communication at all levels. Behind that behavioural matrix detailed above is an assumption that everyone is going to be able and willing to adopt these new behaviours, and the matrix provides the guidebook for everyone to follow. Once the matrix has been communicated, at big picture and detail level, across the organisation, training then needs to be provided to support it.

An analysis of what kind of activities are really behind the behaviours, and what skills are required, leads to a training needs analysis, with different needs at different levels of the organisation. The training could be provided as optional or mandated, depending on how revolutionary the new skillset is.

This training will need to be supported by an internal communications campaign, explaining what training will be provided and how it is supporting the new behaviours. The communications campaign may have to establish a new mindset around certain elements of the required behaviours to overcome all the barriers and fears we have detailed earlier, and that senior management will have already looked at.

An example of this is when the behaviours require what might be described as a difficult conversation. Calling it a difficult conversation will only add to the difficulty, as we mentioned earlier. Running a strong communications campaign around 'critical conversations', for example, may raise the importance of such conversations in the minds of the employees. You might even call them transformational conversations, as we did earlier.

When behaviours are supported by training, and both are supported by a strong communications campaign that overcomes barriers and builds new beliefs, these elements start to provide the framework for all the critical parts in Employee Confidence to blend and work together.

Measure how far you've come

In any system designed to achieve improvement, we need to have a benchmark against which to measure that improvement, and to regularly check how far we have come from that benchmark measure. Since Employee Confidence is a culture change in itself, measuring how employees feel, how much trust they have in themselves and their company, and how willing and able they are to show leadership and realise their true potential, then we need to measure these elements on a regular basis.

We talked about running an Employee Confidence survey right at the beginning of the book, and the final element then of embedding Employee Confidence and making it stick is conducting further surveys to measure the change and communicating the results to employees. It is only by measuring progress that further motivation and guidance will be provided to drive continuous improvement in Employee Confidence.

Measuring progress is the penultimate element in the AABB (Assess, Address, Build, Blend) formula for making Employee

Confidence stick, and is critical in closing the loop in the continuous improvement of the culture change system.

Be ready for exceptional situations

Now we've defined our matrix of behaviours at all levels, and communicated it so everyone knows what they need to do. We've provided training to match the new skillsets required, at all levels of the organisation, and a communication plan to support this. If all goes according to plan, we have a great chance of achieving culture change through Employee Confidence and personal leadership. Inevitably, though, there will be exceptional one-off situations that require a dedicated approach.

Let me give you an example. A project I was asked to advise on was only a few months in duration but the stakes were high – continuous working through three consecutive shifts, complex equipment and machinery, and pressure from the client to complete on time, and with zero defects. We couldn't rely on the existing Quality culture within the company because there would be very few of our own people on site, and the contractor personnel were also relatively unknown to us although they passed all the paper tests. We could have just rolled out our own culture change programme on the project, with the appropriate communication and training, but would we have enough time to make an impact?

In this kind of situation, where we have an additional short-term project where the stakes are high and standards need to be embedded and upheld extremely quickly, we need to take extra measures to get a culture of Employee Confidence established quickly. What we did in this example was to deliver a fast-track training programme at project kick-off, and then embed full-time 'Quality Buddies' as part of the actual workforce, to quickly embed the behaviours taught in the fast-track training. The project was delivered with zero defects and ahead of schedule.

Employee Confidence becomes a firm fixture and fully blended within the organisation when you have a clear definition of the required leadership behaviours at all levels, a training and communications plan to support it, and a readiness to adapt to exceptional one-off situations. And that's when you will start to see a happier, more confident workforce and raised levels of performance.

EMPLOYEE CONFIDENCE RULE 30 – THE AABB FORMULA FOR MAKING EMPLOYEE CONFIDENCE STICK

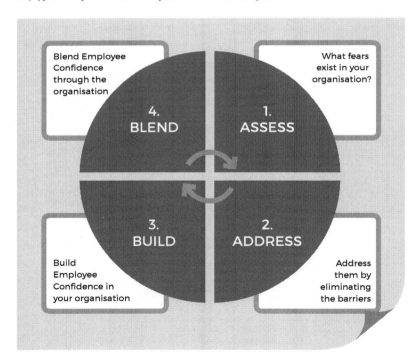

Conclusion

This book has gone beyond Employee Engagement and embraced a new approach – Employee Confidence. And with it a framework for building confidence in our employees and the confident organisation, and for making it stick. We know what Employee Confidence is, why it is important and how to build it. We also know how to bring it to life, through the many Employee Confidence rules peppered throughout the book. Whatever your stake or interest in People, Culture and Behaviours, I sincerely hope you found some value in its pages.

Employee Confidence will transform culture in ways most companies have never even considered, and with results that go far beyond Employee Engagement. Indeed, Employee Confidence is culture change and a culture itself. Other companies will continue to study their ailing engagement figures. You on the other hand will be solving the problem from a whole new level and reaping the rewards that a strong culture always bestows on performance.

Every successful company will need to change culture at some point, or build a new one around an issue of strategic importance. For both scenarios, Employee Confidence is key, giving your employees the skills to help them have critical and even transformational conversations, and in doing so, lead the required change. A few underconfident employees can break your organisation, and many confident employees together will build it up and keep it there.

The time is ripe to invest in Employee Confidence and create ALLPOs, not HIPOs, giving every employee the opportunity to reach full potential, not just the chosen few. Promoting Employee Confidence is the right thing to do and is good for business. With Employee Confidence, you'll leapfrog Employee Engagement and build value in your human capital that will transform company performance and deliver results.

Further reading

For more information and resources on Employee Confidence, please visit: www.leaderlike.co.uk

About the author

Karen J Hewitt is an expert in People, Culture and Behaviours. She holds an MBA with a communication specialism, and is a certified trainer of NLP and Hypnosis. Passionate about the subject of Confidence, and its application in the workplace, she has spent the past seven years observing how confidence, or a lack of it, can be the key ingredient to, and driver of, engagement, culture change and performance. With Employee Confidence – a term she has pioneered in the context of culture change – Karen urges companies to embrace a systems approach to its application and empower their employees to adopt more 'leader-like' behaviours. Through her writing, speaking and training, Karen brings insights into employee and company psychology that will surprise and delight you in equal measure.

Made in the USA
Middletown, DE
08 August 2018